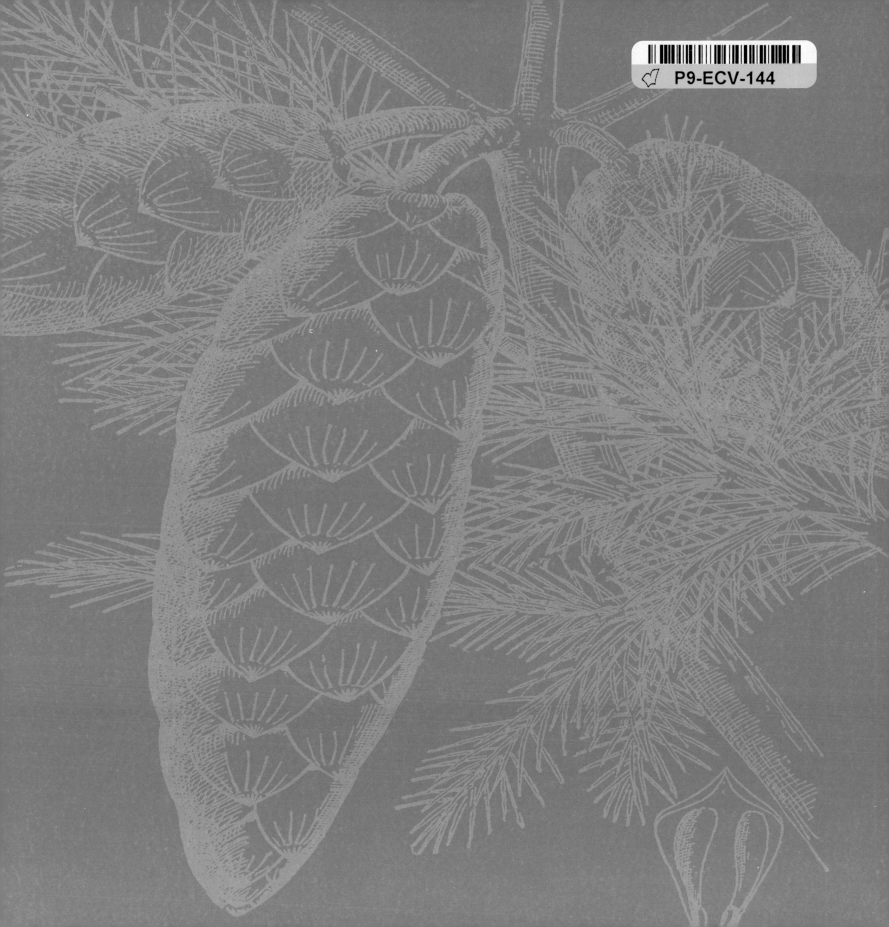

LOG CABIN LIVING

Log Cabin Living

Daniel Mack

GIBBS·SMITH
PUBLISHER

SALT LAKE CITY

This book comes from the vigilant eye of Gibbs Smith, who, after bringing books full of beautiful contemporary log homes into view, wanted to frame the new with the old by adding a historic and poetic dimension to the lure of the log cabin.

It also comes equally from Suzanne Taylor, whose experience in editing and producing books gave her the vision and stamina to help invent this book with designer Scott Knudsen. Both added vitality to magnify my words.

Loren Talbot hunted and gathered beautiful, interesting, useful, and arcane information, while dozens of other log-home lovers responded with quick enthusiasm and generosity in pictures and words.

Log Cabin Living invites reaction and interaction. Please contact us.

Daniel Mack
June 1999

First edition
03 02 01 00 99   5 4 3 2 1

Text copyright © 1999 by Daniel Mack

Published by
Gibbs Smith, Publisher
P.O. Box 667
Layton, Utah 84041

Orders: (1-800) 748-5439
Web site: www.gibbs-smith.com

Edited by Suzanne Taylor
Book design and production by J. Scott Knudsen,
   Park City, Utah
Printed in China

Library of Congress Cataloging-in-Publication Data
Mack, Daniel, 1947–
   Log cabin living / Daniel Mack. — 1st ed.
       p.   cm.
   ISBN 0-87905-920-6
   1. Log cabins. 2. Country life. I. Title.
TH4840.M26   1999   99-30624
690'.873—dc21   CIP

Contents

LOG CABIN DREAMS

Very few of us live in log cabins or will ever build one. But the ideal of the log cabin is the doorway into better understanding the nature of home, dreaming, and the need and fear of solitude, contact with nature, and the past and future.

This book empowers you to **seek out your own log cabin**—that place where things are safe, quiet, and you can just be yourself.

For those who live in log homes, or dream to someday, this book should refine and deepen your appreciation of what you have chosen to do. It will offer some relief from the steady patter of decisions and details needed to get the log home actually done and celebrate the dreamy side of the process that first got you going.

For those of us who are quite happy in our regular houses or apartments but dream about log cabins, this connects us to our need for contact with nature and our changing feelings on the questions of home and hearth.

Every one of us knows about log cabins. It's been in the air we've breathed since we were born. You can be the most dedicated city-bound pansy, but you

"**T**he dream that is dying and the dream that is coming to birth do not stand in sequence, but mingle as do the images in a dissolving view."

—**LEWIS MUMFORD**

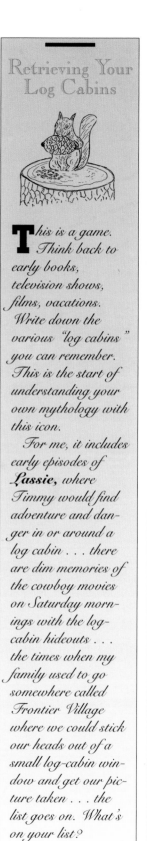

This is a game. Think back to early books, television shows, films, vacations. Write down the various "log cabins" you can remember. This is the start of understanding your own mythology with this icon.

For me, it includes early episodes of **Lassie,** where Timmy would find adventure and danger in or around a log cabin . . . there are dim memories of the cowboy movies on Saturday mornings with the log-cabin hideouts . . . the times when my family used to go somewhere called Frontier Village where we could stick our heads out of a small log-cabin window and get our picture taken . . . the list goes on. What's on your list?

know about log cabins. The log cabin is a rich metaphor in American life. One way to dive beneath the surface of the log cabin is to pay very close attention to the words that are often found with it: "It's my dream." Dream, dream . . . that footloose collection of images, jumps, and lurches bringing with it bits of memories and terrors and pleasures. So the log cabin has something to do with transferring and dreaming. What is going where? A dream is an opportunity to transcend the present moment, to go back and to go ahead.

Often, the dream of the log cabin goes back years, sometimes to childhood. Actually, our childhoods were filled with references to log cabins.

This is the "metaphor" or transferring quality of the log cabin. It's really a big ship to carry dreams.

If this book is worth your time and money, then it should get you moving. It should offer you encouragement to do, to make, to read, to write. It should activate you. Everything in life should do this.

There is a story about Captain Cook visiting the Hawaiian Islands. After coming ashore, Cook pointed

out his great ship to the natives. They could not see it, even though it was only a few hundred yards offshore. Cook then took some of the natives out to the boat and they still couldn't see it until they were actually touching it. The point of the story is that it is very hard to believe and "see" something that is different from the rest of your experience.

I am trying something similar with the log cabin . . . but in reverse. I want to take you up to a log cabin and make it disappear . . . You can't see a log, a notch, a fireplace, a pair of snowshoes . . . All you can see is smoke and mirrors, mists and shadows. Actually, things look better if you squint or look just to the side. And you really get a sense of where

Do you remember the log-cabin project you made in fifth grade?

you are if you close your eyes altogether and listen and smell and remember.

The cabin is a passageway to other places and other ways and other times. That's what we are all looking for anyway, ways to help explain the ancient mysteries of being alive. The log cabin was and still is just a setting for that search to take place and some of those answers or directions to emerge.

This book is a garden where things are planted, but there are already many things dormant in the soil. In time, and with surprises, things emerge and demand of you patience, forbearance, forgiveness . . . and you get rewarded with the beauty you have had a part in bringing to be. Here is your garden bed. You, reader, invest in it with your interests, time, and reactions.

In the process, certain ideas, notions, or pictures will get stuck under the fingernails of your heart and go with you, marking you. After a while, you will begin to select and watch and make the subject matter of this book truly your own. You mark it and charge it with your story. That is the only way it can have any life.

I am not an academic, a historian, a psychologist, or a shop teacher. I do not think you need instruction, help, information, or analysis. You have lived your whole life quite nicely without this book, but what this book can do is what a good restaurant can do. It puts together some unusual choices. You have the right to walk directly out, or you can look over the choices and remark at how simple, interesting, stupid, peculiar, curious, odd, soothing, playful, sweet, romantic, and repulsive it is. In short, in this log-cabin restaurant of stuff, you, like any good customer are treated well and given the choice and support to be brave and try something new, or a new combination of the familiar.

I am an artist, who does not live in a log cabin. My purpose is an artistic one: to move you. The book is about you, not log cabins. If this collection of pictures and drawings and ramblings and excerpts is done correctly, you will be energized in several ways. You will see things differently. This includes how you see yourself. You may come to a new or different appreciation for your talents and interests. You may have renewed interest in family or community. You may want to experiment with altering the pace of activities or scale of activities in your life. You may see "play" in a new way.

After building and making objects for twenty years, I have finally come to realize that I don't really see what I am doing. I can't see what I'm doing because some of it takes place—actually most of it—out of sight. The real life of objects is a multisensual phenomenon. Pictures only tell a thousand of the words. For something to have meaning, it gets sensed by the eyes, by the hands, by the memory, by smell, over time, and by the presence and reaction of animals, birds, and insects. It is sensed by temperature and the gaze of children. In other words, most of the depth of an experience is unseen and unseeable but not unfelt.

Come in and explore the lingering power of the log cabin.

Daniel Mack
Warwick, New York, 1999

Part One

YOU ARE NOT ALONE

istory, like a river, starts in many places: streams, swamps, and springs. Following the log cabin back through time is not a single path but a tangled adventure into geography and the imagination.

THE WOODS: Hey, city boy, how did you get stuck out here in the forest tonight? This isn't the Appalachian Trail or a national park or even a state campground. You are lost and cold and tired. Were you a Boy Scout? No? Well, good luck. Let's see what you do.

THE CITY BOY: Should I huddle under a larch tree? Against the side of a hill? Near some rocks? Will I die . . . ?

These are the dream-terrors that have intrigued explorers both real and imaginary, filling the pages of history.

Laps, Huts, Shanties, and Mansions

*W*e all carry with us the genetic memory of that which has gone before. Each of us, in our own way as similar and special as snowflakes or leaves, formulates the questions and answers to many basic enduring questions. Our moment in civilization, with our technology, is but a flea's breath of human history.

❦ ❦ ❦

Our genetic memories have been formed and rooted in centuries of primitivism. These swampy memories are there. They wait to be addressed. Literature, mythology, religion, and art are ways into and back to them. We need to practice night vision to see them. Look off just to the side of something to see it at night. That's why you can go somewhere else to find out how to build a log cabin or to trace the things. The shadows of the log cabin stretch way back.

When Adam got kicked out of the Garden of Eden, he became the first pioneer. Architectural historians and architects continue to puzzle and speculate over what he did, what he built.

14

The four most
commonly
used trees for
building log homes
are lodgepole pine,
Douglas fir, spruce,
tamarack, or
western larch.

WE TOOK
TO THE
WOODS

Louise Dickinson Rich

*W*e are all Adam. We are all looking for a way back. We are trying to make the wilderness into a garden, to find protection from danger. We want safety, enclosure. As children we hide, we sit on laps, negotiate to get held. Most of us still do this as adults.

As children and adults we also build: under tables, in closets, beneath stairs, or wherever we feel to do so.

A child constructing a den or clubhouse under the hedge is doing far more than merely manipulating dirt and branches. He or she is having a powerful experience of creativity, of learning about self via molding the physical environment.

—**CLARE COOPER MARCUS**
Home as a Mirror of Self

"Backyard" THINGS THAT ARE FUN TO BUILD!

A "Backyard" book by Ray Wallace

HIDING in a FORT

Backyard Retreats for Kids

Lawson Drinkard
Illustrated by Fran Lee

I don't think anyone teaches someone to build like this. There is just a lure to do so.

We hear stories of little people living in the hills, under and in trees. **Hollow trees are magic.** They hold, connect, and hide.

Make a Simple Fort

Grab your mother, father, son, daughter, granddaughter, grandson, niece, or nephew—work with them to make a simple fort out of what you can find in your backyard. How do they see the process? How do they react? What do they begin to see that they never saw before? How does this make them and you feel?

17

s an example of this, a few years ago, I returned to the woods of my boyhood in a rough suburb outside Rochester, New York. Some of the very same woods and trees had remained for the forty years between my visits. In the late 1950s, these woods were home to tree forts, caves, scrap-wood cabins, dugout pit houses, and several other forms of primitive abodes. We often warred with each other, and the houses took much of the beating. Today, forty years later, I found the newest version of the ancient hut—but now the materials of choice included scrap lumber, old shipping pallets, and a plastic tarp. The woods today are still filled with huts and shelters, otherwise known as the laps of trees.

There are log, stick, and natural-form structures all over the forested world, even today. Once in a while they even show up on the front pages of the *New York Times*.

PHOTO COURTESY TERI MACK

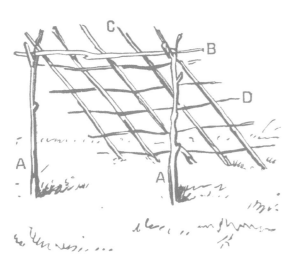

Log cabins are being built by Alpine Log Homes in Montana with an average sticker price of $1.2 million, with options such as indoor pools, movie theaters, and a twelve-car garage.

These are as vital as the early American log cabin: born of necessity, from easy, nearby materials—both disposable or transportable—made with the simplest of tools in the fastest of time. This form of building has survived in our techno-culture in books, in the Boy Scout program, and in the lean-to shelters along the Appalachian Trail. The formulas for making these proto-shelters are so intriguing. Don't you just want to make one in your backyard for the "kids"? Wouldn't it be a great garden "folly" or a potting shed or just a place to look at?

In an 1892 book *Through the Wilds*, Fred, Ned, Dick, and George went to the woods. While Fred went fishing and Dick built a fire, George had Ned help him make a shelter for the night:

"I want a couple of crotched maples or white birches first, Ned, about eight feet long, and, (looking around him) here we have the very thing," pointing to a clump of maples a short distance away. Ned went for them, and soon had the saplings cut down to the right length, and one end of each sharpened. Telling Ned to cut a straight pole about seven feet long, George brought the other two, and selecting a level place near the road, after hard work managed to drive each of the forked sticks a foot into the ground. Ned now came up with the straight one, and this was placed on top of the other two in the crotches. Then they cut seven more about eight feet long; and these George placed one end on the ground and the other end on the top of the horizontal pole and the framework for the camp was finished. On these poles he spread two of the rubber blankets, covering them with boughs, and laid a couple of heavy spruce limbs to keep them in place. If there had been promise of any wind he would have tied them securely to the framework as they had plenty of twine . . .

I'll get back to George and friends as they start to build furniture and do some cooking. But my real hero in primitive shelters is Dan Beard, a gentle, generous man who was one of the founders of the Boy Scouts. In his 1914 book, *Shelters, Shacks, and Shanties*, he spends several chapters leading the pioneer builder out of each of us with his encouraging words and attractive drawings.

20

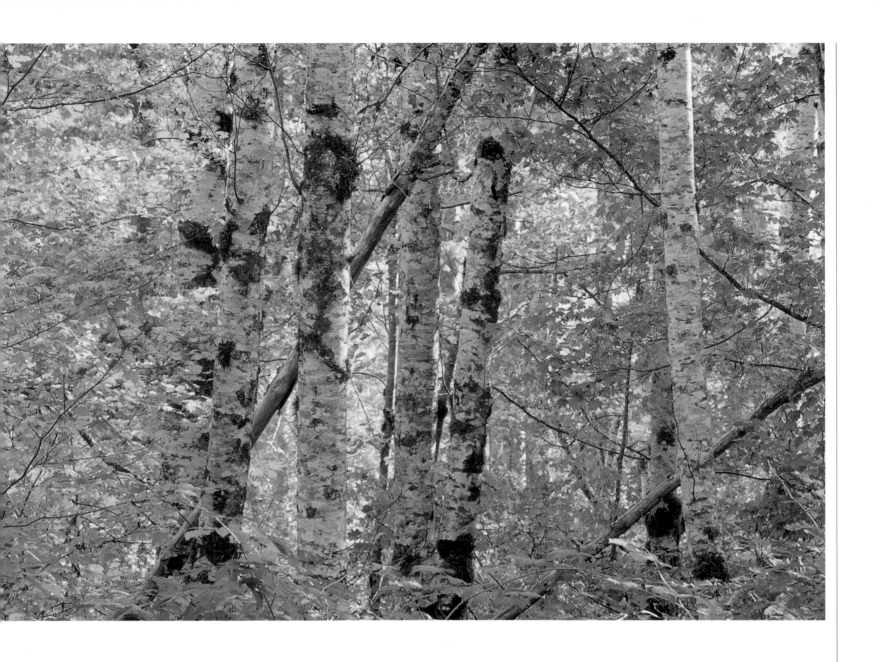

Logs keep the home almost twice as warm as a wood-frame house.

Our Cabin in the Woods

In 1969, my husband Tony and I purchased land in rural Arcade, New York, near the Finger Lakes region, with the desire to have a place to retreat to from our normal, everyday routine—a place where we could enjoy spending time together as a family having picnics and going hiking in the summer, deer hunting in fall, and snowmobiling and cross-country skiing in the winter. It would be a place where we could spend time observing and listening to all the sounds of nature, forgetting, for the moment, all the cares and responsibilities at home.

In 1971, we made a family decision that we needed a place to stay overnight. Our sons, Mark and Dan, were sixteen and fourteen years old. For a family project, we all sat around the kitchen table to draw up plans for a "cabin." The criteria were that it was to be big enough to be comfortable, functional but simple enough to blend in with the natural surroundings of the woods. We decided that the cabin was to be 20 x 32 feet with two bedrooms, one bathroom, a living room with a fireplace, and a kitchenette and needed to cost as little as possible. By the time the project was completed, in addition to our time, we invested a total of $4,000.

We cut down hemlock trees from the property with chainsaws, dragged them out of the woods with a tractor, and had them hauled by truck to a sawmill to be cut into lumber. The exterior of the cabin was constructed of bark-edged hemlock boards, which we thought blended in well with the surrounding woods.

We all participated in building the cabin. We felt

very strongly that our sons should learn about basic construction. Our fourteen-year-old son, Dan, and his father built the fireplace, and Mark and Dan each carved their names with the year the cabin was built in the foundation.

We learned some valuable lessons: the meaning of working together as a family and the importance of cooperation, team effort, compromise, and good work ethics, but most importantly, the satisfaction of accomplishing a worthwhile project that could be enjoyed for many years to come.

When we rose in the morning to watch the sun rise in the east, we would often see whitetail deer out in the field foraging for food along with flocks of wild turkey. Upon opening the door, the songbirds would fill the air with their wonderful soothing melodies. As the gentle winds blew, we could hear the rustling of the leaves on the trees adding their own beautiful music. In the cool summer and fall evenings, many songs were

sung and stories told around a warm campfire. Looking up into the sky, we would bask in the beauty of the universe and count the many stars as well as the many blessings we had received as a family.

This cabin in the woods has served us well. Today, a new family is building memories there. We sold the cabin in 1990, but we still own 80 acres adjacent to the cabin, and in 1991, three generations of Horschels planted 23,000 pine trees as a conservation project to clean the air for future generations. Now our cabin in the woods is the guardian of this newly planted pine woods.

SUZANNE HORSCHEL
South Wales, New York

Log homes were originally built with only an ax or adze and an auger.

NATIVE AMERICAN STRUCTURES

Beard and other woodspeople based much of their work on natural-form structures built by the Native Americans long before the fussy log cabin arrived. The wigwam, the longhouse, the hogan, the pueblo—each had a rich physical and spiritual dimension, more than we are aware of in our houses today. I'll just talk of the one I know most about.

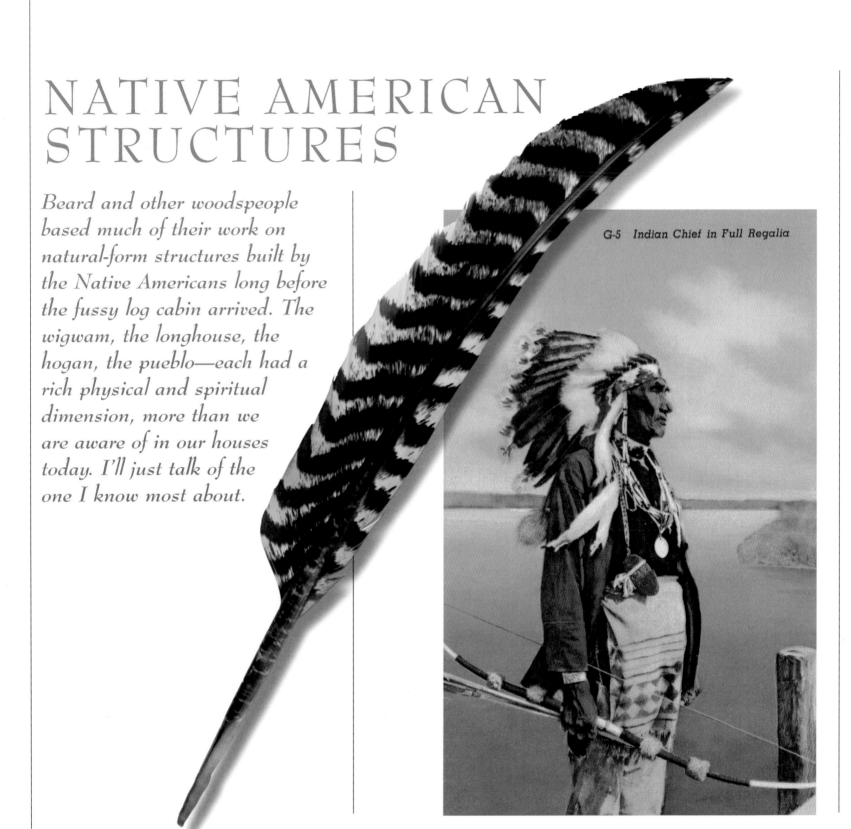

G-5 Indian Chief in Full Regalia

The Longhouse

In western New York State, I grew up learning about the Iroquois Federation—several tribes who farmed, hunted, and fished the fertile Finger Lakes areas. In a clearing, on high ground in the forest, they built villages. There may have been up to twenty longhouses per village, surrounded by fields and stockade fencing. These were no huts. They were described by explorers as fifty feet long, twenty feet wide, and fifteen to twenty feet tall. (Compare this to the later log cabins, which were sometimes ten feet wide by twelve feet long and maybe six feet high!) The longhouses were rectangular and made from poles set in the ground and secured by the inner bark of the slippery elm tree.

936 WATCHING THE SIGNAL FIRE

INDIAN CAMP IN THE MOUNTAINS

2A-H682

The Iroquois also used the thick outer bark of the elm tree as slab shingles over the pole frame of the longhouse. Inside, with openings only on the ends, there lived several families. A cooking fire was shared by families living across from each other. Families slept on low platform lofts and kept their personal belongings beneath. The longhouses, like their later cousins the log cabins, were dark. There were no windows in the sides, just the openings at the ends and the holes in the roof for the smoke.

THOREAU'S CABIN

Most everyone has heard of Henry David Thoreau, a writer and thinker who, in 1845 when he was twenty-seven years old, went to build his own little cabin at the edge of a local pond in Concord, Massachusetts, on the property of his friend and mentor Ralph Waldo Emerson. His purpose was to withdraw just enough from civilization to examine the elements of a simpler life. Indeed, he existed on food he raised himself and kept clear and insightful notes on his experiences. In this way, he was one of the first witnesses to the pull we all still feel to the woods and the simpler life. But Thoreau was seen as quite an odd man in his own time. His writings hardly sold, and after his time alone on Walden Pond, he worked as a local surveyor until he died of tuberculosis at the age of forty-six during the Civil War. He is best known and most remembered for his writings while living at Walden Pond and an essay on civil disobedience. Both have stayed in print to become landmarks of literature. It is not difficult reading as is most nineteenth-century prose. It is enjoyable and lyrical and poetically inspired. It is worth the time to sit and read it. Here is an excerpt from early in the book on how he actually built his one-room cabin:

This is what Thoreau built and lived in for a little over two years. Though he lived in the cabin for that amount of time, his writing in Walden seemed to take place over a one-year period, and he actually took a trip to the wilderness of Maine during this time. For Thoreau, the ideal was neither the savage nor the civilized but to be "half-cultivated."

"Though we are not so degenerate but that we might possibly live in a cave or a wigwam or wear skins today, it certainly is better to accept the advantages, though so dearly bought, which the invention and industry of mankind offer. In such a neighborhood as this, boards and shingles, lime and bricks, are cheaper and more easily obtained than suitable caves, or whole logs, or bark in sufficient quantities, or even well-tempered clay or flat stones. I speak understandingly on this subject, for I have made myself acquainted with it both theoretically and practically. With a little more wit we might use these materials so as to become richer than the richest now are, and make our civilization a blessing. The civilized man is a more experienced and wiser savage. But to make haste to my own experiment.

Near the end of March, 1845, I borrowed an axe and went down to the woods by Walden Pond, nearest to where I intended to build my house, and began to cut down some tall, arrowy white pines, still in their youth, for timber. It is difficult to begin without borrowing, but perhaps it is the most generous course thus to permit

your fellow-men to have an interest in your enterprise. The owner of the axe, as he released his hold on it, said that it was the apple of his eye; but I returned it sharper than I received it. It was a pleasant hillside where I worked, covered with pine woods, through which I looked out on the pond, and a small open field in the woods where pines and hickories were springing up. The ice in the pond was not yet dissolved, though there were some open spaces, and it was all dark-colored and saturated with water. There were some slight flurries of snow during the days that I worked there; but for the most part when I came out on to the railroad, on my way home, its yellow sand-heap stretched away gleaming in the hazy atmosphere, and the rails shone in the spring sun, and I heard

the lark and pewee and other birds already come to commence another year with us. They were pleasant spring days, in which the winter of man's discontent was thawing as well as the earth, and the life that had lain torpid began to stretch itself. One day, when my axe had come off and I had cut a green hickory for a wedge, driving it with a stone, and had placed the whole to soak in a pond-hole in order to swell the wood, I saw a striped snake run into the water, and he lay on the bottom, apparently without inconvenience, as long as I stayed there, or more than a quarter of an hour; perhaps because he had not yet fairly come out of the torpid state. It

appeared to me that for a like reason men remain in their present low and primitive condition; but if they should feel the influence of the spring of springs arousing them, they would of necessity rise to a higher and more ethereal life. I had previously seen the snakes in frosty mornings in my path with portions of their bodies still numb and inflexible, waiting for the sun to thaw them. On the 1st of April it rained and melted the ice, and in the early part of the day, which was very foggy, I heard a stray goose groping about over the pond and cackling as if lost, or like the spirit of the fog. So I went on for some days cutting and hewing timber, and also studs and rafters, all with my narrow axe, not having many communicable or scholar-like thoughts, singing to myself,

Men say they know many things;
But lo! They have taken wings,
The arts and sciences,
And a thousand appliances;
The wind that blows
Is all that anybody knows.

I hewed the main timbers six inches square, most of the studs on two sides only, and the rafters and floor timbers on one side, leaving the rest of the bark on, so that they were just as straight and much stronger than sawed ones. Each stick was carefully mortised so tenoned by its stump, for I had borrowed other tools by this time. My days in the woods were not very long ones; yet I usually carried my dinner of bread and butter, and read the newspaper in which it was wrapped, at noon, sitting amid the green pine boughs which I had cut off, and to my bread was imparted some of their fragrance, for my hands were covered with a thick coat of pitch. Before I had done I had cut down some of them, having become better acquainted with it. Sometimes a rambler in the wood was attracted by the sound of my axe, and we chatted pleasantly over the chips which I had made.

By the middle of April, for I made no haste in my work, but rather made the most of it, my house was framed and ready for the raising. I had already bought the shanty of James Collins, an Irishman who worked on the Fitchburg Railroad, for boards. James Collins' shanty was considered an uncommonly fine one. When I called to see it he was not at home. I walked about the outside, at first unobserved from within, the window was so deep and high. It was of small dimensions, with a peaked cottage roof, and not much else to be seen, the dirt being raised five feet all around as if it were a compost heap. The roof was the soundest part, though a good deal warped and made brittle by the sun. Doorsill there was none, but a perennial passage for the hens under the door-board. Mrs. C. came to the door and asked me to view it from the inside. The hens were driven in by my approach. It was dark, and had a dirt floor for the most part, dank, clammy, and aguish, only here a board and there a board which would not bear removal. She lighted a lamp to show me the inside of the roof and the walls, and also that the board floor extended under the bed, warning me not to step into the cellar, a sort of dust hole two feet deep. In her own words, they were "good boards overhead, good boards all around, and a good window," of two whole squares originally, only the cat had passed out that way lately. There was a stove, a bed, and a place to sit, an infant in the house where it was born, a silk parasol, gilt-framed looking-glass, and a patent new coffee-mill nailed to an oak sapling, all told. The bargain was soon concluded, for James had in the meanwhile returned. I to pay four dollars and twenty-five cents tonight, he to vacate at five tomorrow morning, selling to nobody else meanwhile: I to take possession at six. It were well, he said, to be there early, and anticipate certain indistinct but wholly unjust claims on the score of ground rent and fuel. This he assured me was the only encumbrance. At six I passed him and his family on the road. One large bundle held their all—bed, coffee-mill, looking-glass, hens— all but the cat; she took to the woods and became a wild cat, and, as I learned afterward, trod in a trap set for woodchucks, and so became a dead cat at last.

I took down this dwelling the same morning, drawing the nails removed it to the pond-side by small cartloads, spreading the boards on the grass there to bleach and warp back again in the sun."

HISTORY 201

The very first shelters made by the European settlers in America in 1620 were lean-tos, wigwam-like structures, probably borrowed from the Native Americans. Other recorded structures of the same time were caves dug into the sides of hills and the shallow pits surrounded by upright posts.

The log cabin didn't appear until the Swedes and Finns came to the U.S. in 1638. Theirs was a truly better idea so appropriate for the forest-rich new world. The log cabin solved the problem of shelter and disposing of the logs on the cleared land. The various ethnic groups who came in contact with the Finns and Swedes appropriated the structure and modified it a bit according to their ethnic traditions. Even the Native Americans saw the value of the log cabin and became adept at its construction.

There was the quick cabin, often taking no more than a few days to erect. This was no log home. It was probably no bigger than the available logs, maybe 15' x 20' at the largest and maybe only 10' x 10'. These logs may not have been hewn but were notched on the ends only. The roof was made from panels of bark. The chinking between the logs was a mixture of mud, moss, and sticks, which fell out every so often. There weren't any windows, and if a fireplace hadn't yet been built, there was an open fire on the floor with the smoke filling the cabin and venting out the door. The floor was just an earth floor. If the cabin became more permanent, the roof may have been replaced with shingles or shakes; the floor may have had half-round logs called "puncheons" put over the packed dirt floor and a window or two might have been cut.

These are pretty rough places. They appeared in American history before the major impact of the Industrial Revolution and would be recognizable to natives many places in the world. But by the turn of the twentieth century, there had been more change in the devices and inventions of domestic life than at any other time in history. Within a decade, the expectations of most Americans for controlled heat and cooling, hot and cold running water, showers, baths, electricity, and a mushrooming number of machines

was beyond the imagination of just an earlier generation. We are living in that time. It is almost impossible for us to understand what creature comforts were in the last centuries. These are places we might visit at a Williamsburg or simulate during mountain-man days, or approximate on a yearly camping trip. We have passed the days of the primitive log cabin.

Historian Lewis Mumford seems to dismiss an interest in certain parts of the past as "little more

than the phosphorescence of decay." By that, I assume he means our eye is caught for a moment by the fading twinkle of a phenomenon in its last stage of demise. Well, isn't that what compost is? Decay transforming into rich support. I think Mumford stops appreciating the phosphorescence too soon. It's a beacon alerting us to the way to look and the way to go. That's my interest in the log cabin. I see its phosphorescence and it helps me see.

Can you trace a log cabin in your family tree? Call your relatives, look through old pictures, read family histories. You might be pleasantly surprised.

PIONEERS

Just Who Were These People?

To many people, those who have and build log cabins and homes are considered pioneers. In the past, they were called borderers, woodboys, squatters, land pirates, back settlers, and finally backwoodsmen. The pioneer, perhaps even more than the log cabin, has stayed in the pith of the American imagination. Depending on who you read, log-cabin pioneers were either brave and noble adventurers or rowdy, irreverent misfits. I think they were and are both. They were young, impelled out of Europe by troubles, and drawn to America by indistinct hopes; they were optimists.

Copyright 1899, by D. R. Kin
Sedro-Woolley, Wash.

32

Terry Jordan, a cultural geographer, has studied the literature and history of the American frontier. He has written three books (see Resources) and has identified characteristics of frontier people shared by many of us today.

Jordan states that America's pioneers had disdain for centralized social institutions like schools, churches, courts, and deed offices. Their settlements were not towns or villages but scattered homesteads, and they valued personal freedom and the rights of the individual above all. The family and extended family was the basic group. There was considerable mixing and intermarriage with Native Americans, and, as a result, shelters, foods, and other parts of daily living were influenced by this.

Cabins were built quickly with the simplest of notched logs that could be taken apart and reconfigured for another building or in another place. Pioneers moved often and followed the guise that if one could see the smoke from a neighbor it was time to move. With the moving came a reliance on hunting and fishing, not agriculture; that was for settlers. There was also little or no concern for conservation because the abundance of the land was overwhelming.

The frontier diet was rich in fatty protein, consisting mostly of pork and wild game with lots of corn breads and alcohol. This resulted in people keeping livestock—especially hogs.

To people from urban society, these woodsboys must have been alien, repulsive, and terrifying. In many of the journals of the day, there was clear disgust and revulsion for these people and their living conditions. This was, by European standards, a vast empty wilderness. It's estimated that at the start of the eighteenth century, there were only about three million Native Americans on the entire American continent. Europe, which was half the size at that time, had 100 million people. Native Americans didn't have towns or cities, which made them even more strange and "invisible" to the Europeans. It was as if Europeans had encountered prehistory.

Forests

America was a land of truly great forests. To the Europeans, that meant far more than timber, game, and land. It was terrifying. The forest is the opposite of civilization. It is indicative of raw disorder, with trees that tower so far above the puny human; the darkness of the forest shades man from the light of God. The opening lines of *Dante's Inferno*:

"In the middle of the journey of our life
I came to myself in a dark wood
where the straight way was lost."

Being on the verge called for special skills and attitudes better suited to some of the new immigrants. Lucy Lockwood Hazard describes the qualities needed as "determination, endurance, independence, ingenuity, flexibility, individualism, and optimism."

Another Log Cabin Game

Think of news stories, television shows, and films of the last few years. Who lives in log cabins? Psychopaths, misfits, bombers...?

Some early cabins were chinked with clay and pig's blood.

VERGES AND BORDERS

Daniel Boorstin introduces a quaint and helpful idea for better understanding the nature of the pioneers. He describes America as a continent of verges. These are the edges between the known and unknown, the familiar and the strange. Much of European history and tradition had been shrouded in the certainty of what was known. Columbus, Boorstin says, was certain he would reach Asia and actually died unaware and unwilling to accept that he had discovered a New World. He describes Columbus as a discoverer, an expert at uncovering what is known to be there.

Pioneers who bound the country shore to shore and Americans today were and are explorers, people who venture into the unknown. Again, in the previous history of Europe, the unknown was also the place of evil, the dark, the forbidden. The great forests were the abode of the devil, wood giants who copulated at will, thieves, dwarfs, misfits, and lunatics, to name a few.

The log cabin appears and reappears many times in our history. Each time it's never quite the same, yet it's still the cabin. This is testament to the power of the icon of the cabin. Regardless of the specific circumstances, the cabin means something primary and connected. Usually something more distant and disconnected has pestered. This rhythm between the one and the other is important to look at. It is part of the necessary polarities. Between the polarities is the edge, the border, "the verge," as Boorstin called it.

John Berger celebrates it a bit differently: "There are truths which can be 'unconcealed' and uncovered in the folds between cultures and epochs."

The log cabin is the first and perhaps temporary shelter we use when we're exploring a verge. It actually indicates that we are on or near a verge or frontier or fold. Looking at today's log cabins, there seem to be several verges, several frontiers.

Abe Lincoln–style cabins weren't popular until the middle of the nineteenth century.

35

LOG CABINISM

Look closely at this engraving from 1883. This is a plan for a rustic summerhouse. There on the horizon line to the left is civilization, the main house. The rustic needs the urban. *Rus et urbe.*

 ome log cabinism is an out-and-out rejection of the urban industrial world, but most people just want relief from the everyday routine. The pioneers used whatever technologies they could to move ahead. They were not fleeing or rejecting the city as much as extending the reach of industrial America. Soon after they explored and pioneered, the settlers followed. For the pioneers, it was time to move if you could see the smoke from a neighbor's chimney. It was also time to move when you had exhausted the game or land in your area.

36

In a very elementary way, the pioneers needed the settlers; the wilderness exists only because it's not the city. The log cabin is refreshing because the city is so stimulating. They are foils for each other, not even really opposites. Vitality doesn't come from a particular place but from a brisk shift or movement, from a feeling of dullness to a feeling of being alive. Soul comes from movement.

Log Cabins and Wars

Sometimes there were actually log block-houses so thick and tightly made that the arrows, bullets, and fires of the enemy could not penetrate. They were forts and fortresses and have remained that way in child's play.

Brown Co. Jail

The log cabin was also the place men fled to *after* the war. The mixed-up backwardness of the Vietnam War sent my generation to the woods. Certainly the rustic revival, which is still in full swing, began during Vietnam. And the rise in all forms of log homes, handcrafted and kits, began as the Vietnam War was ending.

Looking farther back to the two world wars, there is literature just after each war that supports and encourages the return to nature.

After World War I, there was considerable literature on woodcraft and camping, both fiction and nonfiction. None was more inviting than the work of Dan Beard, who started the Boy Pioneers of America and finally merged them with the Camp-Fire Club into the Boy Scouts. He wrote for boys of all ages deliberately including the older boys who are called scoutmasters or sportsmen. The quiet fraternity of scouts even today has a deep pull on Americans. These scouts were benign Indians, skilled in old-woods ways as well as the challenges of the modern world. Again, there was the fusion of the raw and the tamed, the rural and industrial. Looking at the merit badges in a Boy Scout handbook is an adventure in time travel and cultural fusion.

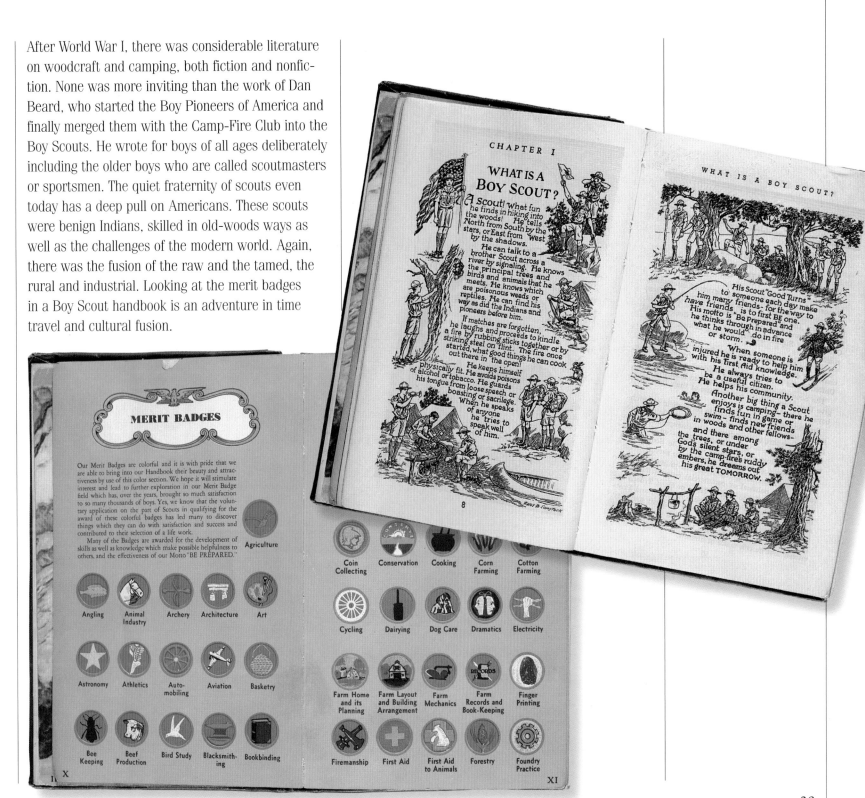

ertainly the demands of a rapidly developing industrial nation created stress. One of Robert Frost's lesser-known poems, "A Lone Striker" (1921), addresses this tension:

The swinging mill bell changed its rate
To tolling like the count of fate,
And though at that the tardy ran,
One failed to make the closing gate,
There was a law of God or man
That on the one who came too late
The gate for half an hour be locked,
His time be lost, his pittance docked.
He stood rebuked and unemployed.
The straining mill began to shake.
The mill, though many, many eyed,
Had eyes inscrutably opaque;
So that he couldn't look inside
To see if some forlorn machine
Was standing idle for his sake.
(He couldn't hope its heart would break.)

And yet he thought he saw the scene:
The air was full of dust of wool.
A thousand yarns were under pull,
But pull so slow, with such a twist,
All day from spool to lesser spool,
It seldom overtaxed their strength;
They safely grew in slender length.
And if one broke by any chance,
The spinner saw it at a glance.
The spinner still was there to spin.

That's where the human came in.
Her deft hand showed with finger rings
Among the harp-like spread of strings.
She caught the pieces end to end
And, with a touch that never missed,
Not so much tied as made them blend.
Man's ingenuity was good.
He saw it plainly where he stood,
Yet found it easy to resist.

He knew another place, a wood,
And in it, tall as trees, were cliffs;
And if he stood on one of these,
'Twould be among the tops of trees,
Their upper branches round him wreathing,
Their breathing mingled with his breathing.
If—if he stood! Enough of ifs!
He knew a path that wanted walking;
He knew a spring that wanted drinking;
A thought that wanted further thinking;
A love that wanted re-renewing.
Nor was this just a way of talking
To save him the expense of doing.
With him it boded action, deed.

The factory was very fine;
He wished it all the modern speed.
Yet, after all, 'twas not divine,
That is to say, 'twas not a church.
He never would assume that he'd
Be any institution's need.
But he said then and still would say
If there should ever come a day
When industry seemed like to die
Because he left it in the lurch,
Or even merely seemed to pine
For want of his approval, why,
Come get him—they knew where to search.

So these threads of war and industry mingle with moments of personal trauma—sickness, death, divorce, fire—to push some people to flee to the verge and take up living in a log cabin of sorts.

Cedar and cypress are natural repellants for bugs, fungus, and rot.

ANOTHER, GENTLER KIND

Many of the people building or acquiring log cabins are older. They are pioneering not real space but time and life cycle. Their cabins are outposts in their own lives, signaling an exploration of a new terrain in the life cycle.

As life expectancy has risen, the notion of retirement is coming to be replaced by what Gail Sheehy calls redirection. Loafing, golfing, and traveling are not enough. There's often too much time left in life after retirement. The cabin, in whatever form, becomes the launch point, the base camp, for the next ascent. Sometimes it's the long-awaited way to simplify and reduce the bulk of possessions and obligations; sometimes it's a way of rebuilding a nest for returning children and grandchildren. Within the next twenty-five years, 20 percent of the American population will be over sixty-five years of age. That creates a situation unparalleled in human history. We need all the pioneers we can find!

OF LOG CABINISM

Read Gail Sheehy's *Understanding Men's Passages: Discovering the New Map of Men's Lives*. It is a clear and steady guide, for both men and women, into the rethinking and repositioning required in extended living.

TECHNO-LOG CABINISM

With the changes in technology, the trend of ten years ago to the electronic cottage and telecommuting has matured, particularly with the internet, into electronic homesteading, where small specialty businesses can be physically located in the country. Certainly, my colleagues in the arts and crafts are pioneering this as they invent their pots and glass and furniture and bring it to the cities or the trading bazaars known as craft fairs. The internet is quickly providing the addresses of these pioneers.

PHOTO COURTESY
JONATHAN WALLEN

Fifty years ago, Conrad Meinecke, in his book *Your Cabin in the Woods*, sketched this as a possibility:

Personally, I believe we will yet trek from the big cities back to the country. There will be smaller cities wherein smaller factories may employ five hundred or a thousand men who, after the day's work is over, may quickly return to their homes and garden plots—men who through eight tedious hours of screwing on nuts and bolts, can still find life, liberty, and the pursuit of happiness on their own half acre in the early morning, after supper, and weekends.

It may not have worked out exactly that way, but America is in its fifth big historical migration. Suburban growth stopped in 1970. "The dream is now elsewhere." Jack Lessinger of the University of Washington estimates that by 2010, probably half of the middle class in the U.S. and Canada will live outside either metropolitan or suburban areas. There is a return to the rural areas, reversing a trend that started about 1848.

Futurist John Naisbett actually invokes the language of the frontier, referring to "the first settlers in the new heartland" as the largely self-employed people who seem to share an uncanny resemblance to the original pioneers. Just as the first pioneers were cut free from Europe, the passing of lifelong job security has led many people to reconsider very fundamental structures in their lives. When this is coupled with better health care, increases in life expectancy, and the idea of retirement implying redirection, there seems to be a whole new wave of pioneers over fifty years of age "westering" their way into new social and cultural wildernesses.

45

THE GREAT CAMPS

I n the 1880s and '90s, as the pioneers were just reaching the West Coast and the frontier of land was closing, several streams of American culture began to merge into what would be called the great camp era—a fifty-year episode that had a lasting influence on the way the log cabin was seen.

Camp Weonah.

The decades after the Civil War were ones of exceptional prosperity in America. It was a moment of financial and cultural maturation. Industry had developed and was expanding on the waves of immigrant labor. There was a homegrown, newly wealthy American aristocracy that began seeking the material honors due their position. Mansions were built along Fifth Avenue in New York City, and many of the major American cultural institutions, like the Metropolitan Museum and the Metropolitan Opera, which now seem so ancient, were freshly endowed. There was travel and the development of multiple residences.

The Adirondacks had long been a mysterious, rough, and inhospitable area. There were very long winters, and the spring and fall were wet. Oh, there were a few great days each summer, but much of the attraction was the unpredictability of the wilderness and the chance to encounter nature.

This was quite different from the experience of the pioneer, who was all too aware of encounters with nature and was threatened and not charmed at all by its powers. Initially, a kind of rugged tourism called "New York fever" developed around the Adirondacks. Behind the tourism was a deeper interest in the timber and the mines of the Adirondacks—and it was all so close! It was only about 200 miles from New York City and on the edge of the rest of New England. After the Civil War, the railroad started penetrating the north woods, and by the 1890s what had been a trek inland via stagecoach over log-embedded roads was almost accessible by railroad. This spurred the development of more hotels and more tourists.

The railroads also owned huge parcels of land. It was on one of these parcels that the son of a railroad developer started building what came to be known as the great camps. About forty camps were built, the earliest in 1878 and the last of the era, Minnowbrook, in 1949. It was money before the institution of income tax that fueled the building, and it was the depression that almost ground it to a halt.

What Is a Great Camp?

A "camp" is a kind of modest term for anything from a shelter of fresh-cut boughs to a log mansion with servants outnumbering guests. But a **great camp** would be an impressive architectural structure, solving masterful problems of comfort and elegance with the use of mostly natural materials, probably obtained locally. It is often a privately built and controlled village of several buildings on hundreds of acres of private land.

The decorations and furnishings gyrate between the homespun and the exotic to the eccentric. It is a place quite hard to get to, and when you are there, notions of time and beauty are altered. There is always some reminder and presence of the civilized world, so it is both quiet and busy as well as natural and unnatural. That is what makes it truly great, its *contra natura*. One current owner says that the purpose of the great camp was to create "the improbable, if not the impossible." That took form in the vision of a shrewd dreamer, William West Durant, the son of a very successful American railroad builder. Durant was educated and lived in Europe until he returned to the United States in 1874 to help develop the Adirondacks with his father. In 1879, he started expanding his father's Camp Pine Knot with local labor and local materials. He was a self-trained architect who actually only designed and built three camps—Pine Knot, Uncas, and Sagamore—but he defined the style in which dozens of others were built. In 1901, nearly bankrupt, he sold off his own great camp, Sagamore, to Alfred Vanderbilt for $162,500. Certainly Durant's social connections to the wealthiest

The Chine, Shanklin I.o.W.

William West Durant's Great Camp, Sagamore.

51

View in Central Park, N. Y.

people in America offered the opportunity for the level of support required by the vision of these camps. But as a designer and builder, Durant was skilled, like the pioneers themselves, at borrowing and adapting features appropriate for the environment.

The use of bark covering and log structures had long been part of the folk and Indian cultures of the area. Great camps came to be known for a strung-out series of separate buildings. This was a feature of the earlier and ubiquitous logging camps where separate buildings meant safety from the spread of fire.

Durant, who lived until 1934, did not build any more camps after the sale of Sagamore, but he worked managing hotels in the Adirondacks region. To put it briefly, the American great camp idiom was fathered by a temporarily wealthy, energetic dreamer who had hardly lived in

America and spent his old age in obscurity.

I speed up this history to make the point that there is *never* a full retreat to the woods. We do live in a global village where lines of interconnection and the six degrees of separation are quite real. The histories of logs in America are tied with cheap land deals with Native Americans; wily emigrant Irish, Scandinavian, and French Canadian loggers; and New Industrialists watching the lovely English-inspired rustic structures go up before their eyes in Central Park, just across the street from their mansions.

Oh, did I forget to mention all the traveling people had done? They included grand tours of the continent to Switzerland and its chalets, and visits to the various exhibitions and world's fairs where the tastes for the Asian and the tribal were developed and later indulged in the camp decor. The camps were and still are quite remote, not unlike movie-stars' homes. They were and are third, fourth, or fifth homes for people. Log cabins are distant poor cousins to these great camps.

Because of their extravagance, the great camps helped bring and lock the idiom of the log cabin into the public consciousness. They are like a great movie or a dream, some fetching an unforgettable, larger-and-faster-than-life mix of unreality. They became the reference point, the cliché. How many of us can afford to build or even stay a few nights in a great-camp type of lodge? But everyone of us can see the pictures, gasp at the scale, feel the dreams, and go away with a little richer sense of fantasy and play. In this way, the great camps feed us the rarest of nourishment—food for our imaginations. We are fed both by the stories of the feats of conception, construction, and craftsmanship and by their pending demise through decay and fire. The great camps embody a very old human story about reaching and soaring and falling. It's about ambition, recognition, and change. We, the rabble, enjoy such stories. Shakespeare taught us well about appearance and reality . . . and other great themes that get played out every day all around us. So the great camps took the simple, rough, inhospitable log cabin and made it the doorway for dreamers. It became a vision of a heaven on earth: a warm, comforting image of nature and appliances and servants taking care of man. This was quite different from the sometimes beautiful but generally threatening face of nature that pioneers and other woodspeople knew all too well. But the great camp image was quite well suited to a population who was more and more tied to the cities, with vacations as the opportunities to experience nature.

COPYRIGHT 1905
J. TULLY

C-23.

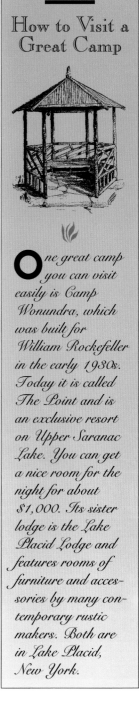

Perhaps the single most important image from the time of the great camps is the photograph of Mrs. Garvan's bed in Camp Kill Kare. Most rustic makers have been asked to make that bed or something that resembles it many times over. This bed captures the fantasy-utility flavor of the great camps themselves as well as rustic furniture. It's an ambiguous object in a room bigger than any of us live in. It is both a tree and a piece of furniture; it is terrifying and pleasing, ugly and attractive, compelling and repelling.

To achieve something appropriately ambiguous is a true feat. It is another of those sought-after moments when the hidden dimensions of reality become evident. It is that Irish resistance to a clear answer: "It is and it isn't" or "It will and it won't." It took me years to understand that this is not an evasion of clarity but a clarification of the

On the Bridge
where the Rivers meet.

way life is.

Whether he meant to or not, Durant and his three great camps started rustic motion in many directions that almost everyone of us can still feel today.

The great camps and the work of William West Durant inspired generations of architects and their wealthy clients. In 1911, furniture designer and writer Gustav Stickley celebrated the log home in the following article and photographs of his own showcase log home at Craftsman Farms in Morris Plains, New Jersey. Stickley seemed to intend the house to be both his residence and the center structure of a school for citizenship, a kind of farm and education camp for boys. Stickley remembered his own youth on the farm in Wisconsin and attributed much of his well-being to a balance of head, heart, and hand. For reasons still unknown, the school never opened and the entire property was sold when Stickley went bankrupt in 1917.

Camp Kill Kare and Mrs. Garvan's bed was one of the most extraordinary examples of rustic construction. One post is fashioned by a tree with an owl perched on its branches and its footboard serves as the backrest of a rustic bench.

*W*hat is there about a log cabin that appeals to our imagination, that seems so alluring and full of the suggestion of romance? The new log house at Craftsman Farms seems to visualize this question, for it is a log cabin idealized. Though adapted to the demands of modern civilization it yet has the charm of the more primitive dwelling and creates the same suggestion of simple and natural living and kinship with the outdoor world. While retaining its dignity of architecture it invites a sense of informality, of intimacy. Here the visitor feels instinctively and immediately at home.

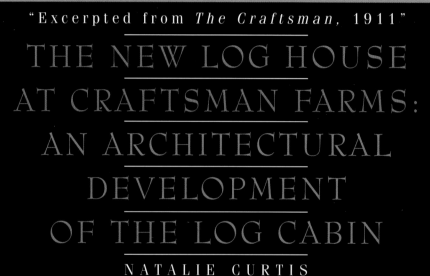

"Excerpted from *The Craftsman, 1911*"

THE NEW LOG HOUSE AT CRAFTSMAN FARMS: AN ARCHITECTURAL DEVELOPMENT OF THE LOG CABIN

NATALIE CURTIS

Seated on the broad veranda with the fields below and the hills beyond, the guest tries to analyze the unconscious fascination of the log cabin which in this building seems intensified by the conscious art of the architect. He looks from the giant beams to the living trees and the forest seems to tell the answer to his thoughts: The house of logs appeals to us because it is a part of our heredity. It was a primitive home to man, a rudimentary sheltering of domestic life, a place of safety where love and friendship could be shut in and foe and danger shut out. The early homes of our Germanic ancestors were huts in the forest sometimes built around a central tree which grew up through the roof and spread its sheltering branches over the dwelling. We came from the forest, and trees formed our home and our protection. And so today a house built of wood which has not been metamorphosed into board and shingle but still bears the semblance of the tree rouses in us the old instinctive feeling of kinship with the elemental world that is a natural heritage.

To us in America the log cabin seems a near friend. For many of us it was the home of our immediate ancestors and it forms a vital part of the life of the white man in this continent. What a train of historical reminiscence the mere thought of the log cabin awakens: the landing of the first settlers, the unbroken wilderness of the primeval forests, the clearing of the ground, the building of the first

homes. How great must have been the need of the comfort of the hearth and the strength of fellowship in that lonely and desperate struggle against the elements, the foe and starvation. Scattered far over this continent, moving northward, southward and westward, the log cabin has been the pioneer of civilization, the sign of the determination of the white man to face the unknown and to conquer all obstacles. Viewed in this light it seems of a certain poetic significance that Lincoln, one of the greatest of the nation's leaders, should have been born and reared in a log cabin.

Since the log house has played so important a part in our history its

development into a definite and characteristic type of architecture might give us something national, something peculiarly American in suggestiveness. Of the distinction and charm of such a type the log house at Craftsman Farms is a proof. Besides, there are elements of intrinsic beauty in the simplicity of a house built on the log cabin idea. First, there is the bare beauty of the logs themselves with their long lines and firm curves. Then there is the open charm of the structural features which are not hidden under plas-

ter and ornament, but are clearly revealed—a charm felt in Japanese architecture which is, as Cram has said, "The perfect style in wood as Gothic is the perfect style in stone." The Japanese principle: "The wood shall be unadorned to show how beautiful is that of which the house is made" is true of the Craftsman development of the log house. For in most of our modern houses "ornament by its very prodigality becomes cheap and tawdry" and by contrast the quiet rhythmic monotone of the wall of logs fills one with the rustic peace of a secluded nook in the woods.

The log cabin type of house seems of all others most fitted for this hospitable Craftsman home. It invites rest in that it seems in itself just a part of the wooded hillside, the human element in the life of forest and field. There is nothing about it that can remind one of street and city, it only deepens the sense of glad release from tension and artificiality.

But now let us consider in detail the interesting features of this house. As in pioneer days, so here, the space for the house had first to be cleared in the forest. The abundant chestnut trees were cut down

and of them the house is built. The logs are hewn on two sides and peeled and the hewn sides laid together. (If the logs are not peeled worms are apt to get behind the bark and work their way through because of the dampness of the wood. The danger is not so great if the wood is dry.) The logs are then "chinked" with cement mortar, which is then mixed in the proportion of two parts sharp sand to one part cement. As far as has been tested this cement mortar adheres perfectly to the wood and makes an absolutely tight joint.

Where the logs cross at the corners they are halved and laid over each other, projecting about a foot. The logs are stained with a Craftsman preparation of wood-oil in which a little brown is mixed to give the peeled wood the color of the tree trunk.

A stone foundation runs under the whole building supporting the great veranda fourteen feet wide which stretches the entire length of the front of the

house. This veranda, swept by every passing breeze, nestling amid the green of the hillside, seems like a vast outdoor living room. There seems space enough here for everything and everybody, and hammocks, books, tables and comfortable chairs tempt one to read, work and play in the open air. At Craftsman Farms there is no excuse for remaining within doors.

A wall two feet wide runs around the veranda, with a door at each end. From the wall rise posts, hewn so slightly that the form still suggests the living

tree. These posts support the ceiling of the veranda, which is the floor of the front rooms on the second story. The floor beams, which thus form the ceiling on the verandas, are from six to eight inches in diameter, hewn straight on one side to receive the floor foundation, which is of two-inch hemlock plank V-jointed. Over the planks are spread layers of thick paper or deafening felt and on top of this is laid the finished floor of regular maple flooring, tongued and grooved.

Of the veranda furniture one of the most interesting bits, from a practical standpoint, is a box thirty inches deep and eighteen inches high, which is made in two sections and forms a combination bench and wood box. In this is kept the smaller wood for the fires.

Most attractive is the cement flooring with its note of color in the border. The foundation of the floor is filled with stone and rubble, the cement is then laid over it. The border is formed of six rows of red bricks placed on edge with wide joints of black cement. The floor is laid in two panels, divided by the border; each panel slopes very slightly to its center, in which is a drain so that the floors can be cleaned with a hose.

Leaving the veranda we enter by a wide door into the great living room. We pause on the threshold, stirred by a dim feeling of the Long Ago. There is something nobly barbaric in the massive rough-hewn

posts supporting the stout beams overhead, the two great hearths with their copper hoods, the crude beauty of the natural wood and the glint of color in the dull orange hangings. From the bare and primitive structure we might fancy ourselves in some tribal hall on the Rhine in the early days of Germanic history; we could imagine *Wappen,* shields and lances, hanging from the great posts; we think involuntarily of the sagas of the North, of "Niebelungen Lied" and of the poems of William Morris. Yet when we step inside and find ourselves surrounded by the comforts and the culture of modern civilization, the rustic setting seems but to deepen the homelike charm of the room and to offer the welcome of old and familiar association.

To return to details, we are first struck by the size of the room which, like the veranda, runs across the whole length of the house. There is a fireplace at each end, corresponding to the two end doors of

the veranda. The great hearths, which have special ventilating appliances, are built of field stone gathered on the place and are topped with low-hanging hoods on which are embossed appropriate mottoes in quaint lettering.

The keystones of the arches over the hearths support the ends of the enormous central ceiling log which runs straight through the middle of the room from hearth to hearth, upheld by three posts. This beam is in reality composed of three logs spliced to

look like one; but the illusion is complete.

In spite of their refinement and detail, the table in the center of the room with lamps and books and the piano in its appropriate Craftsman case harmonize perfectly with the harsher accents of the log structure which is stained the same brown as the furniture. Most of the available wall space is filled by bookcases whose volumes offer a background of dull diffuse color which helps to soften the crudity of the wood. Above the bookcases and over the settles are windows with many small diamond-panes, which form a happy contrast to the heavy horizontal lines of the structure and relieve the massiveness of the logs by an effect of delicacy. The light is softened to a mellow glow by casement curtains of burnt orange with a border worked in appliqué linen.

On the floor are handmade Drugget rugs of bullock-wool, imported from India. These rugs are green, relieved by a design of pale grey, and they harmonize with the wood trimmings and the oak staircase, which are stained leaf-green.

The color scheme of the whole room reminds one of the forest—brown and green with the glint of sunshine through the leaves, suggested by the gold of the windows and the gleaming of copper in the hearthhoods, the door-latches and the vases and bowls on the bookcase and table.

The dining room runs parallel to the living room.

Here also is a big ventilating hearth. These fireplaces heat the entire house with hot water and warm air. The color scheme in the dining room is much the same as in the living room, except that the rugs are brighter in tone, being hand-made Donegal Irish rugs in which a yellow design blends with green. A long sideboard with drawers and cupboard bears the weight of copper candlesticks and table furniture.

Beyond the dining room is the kitchen, a large room, light and airy, with a huge range capable of cooking for a hundred people. There are special appliances for convenience in washing dishes and excellent stationary tubs. The kitchen is painted a cool white.

The main rooms on the second floor are at the two ends of the house; one of them, a bedroom, is furnished and decorated in yellow and seems aglow with sunshine; the other, a much larger bedroom, is done in blue and gray. This latter room has a peculiar charm because of its woodwork of dark gumwood, which is perhaps as beautiful as any produced by Craftsman design. The color scheme has a certain feminine refinement. The walls are covered with gray Japanese grass-cloth and the hearth is of dull blue Grueby tiles with a brass hood. The furniture is gray oak, decorated with a small design inlaid with blue and copper. This design is outlined in black and is crossed by a delicate vine-like figure of greenish yellow. Unlike those bedrooms in which "daintiness" is expressed by

weakness, tawdry trimmings, flippancy and ruffles, this room has both delicacy and strength and is thus appropriate to the ideal of the modern woman.

The log house at Craftsman Farms expresses that simple sincerity that is part of the Craftsman ideal. It charms the visitor by its harmony with nature and its unity of the best in civilization with the best in cruder forms of life. To the strength, the courage and the honest effort typified by the primitive log cabin, art has here added the grace of beauty, and science the requisites of comfort.

Use of Logs in Building

Logs destined to be used in the building of a home should be cut in the winter and the bark removed. They should be well seasoned before being used in the construction of a house so that the possibility of shrinking, warping or loosening of the chinking will be avoided. A house can be made with the logs standing on end or in a horizontal position, but in either case they should be dressed on two sides so that they may fit together better. The inside and outside of each log should be left round that the grace in the curve of the log may be retained.

The fitting of the logs at the corners when they are to be used in the old-time horizontal way must be carefully done when each log is ready to be laid in position. The irregularity of the logs demands very careful measuring for the halving of the corners. The logs are pinned together at the corners with wooden

pins about an inch in diameter. If the logs are very long, if the house is to be a large one, wooden pins are used occasionally between the corners to hold the logs firmly together.

After the walls have been built up then they are pointed with cement mortar, which makes a permanent and a tight solid wall. This cement chinking can be stained to match the timbers so that one even tone can be obtained for the whole exterior or interior of the house.

A more modern and satisfactory way to build a house of logs is to place them in a horizontal position. This is a more simple form of construction and so could be undertaken by those not experienced in log house building. The difficult process of plumbing the corners of the building and the tying together of the logs is eliminated in this method. The logs are stood on end on sills and held at the top by a plate through which wooden pins are driven into each log. The inequality of the logs holds the cement chinking in place and thus a substantial and decidedly artistic wall is obtained. The logs can be waterproofed and preserved by the application of wood oil, and if desired stain can be added to this oil, which will render logs and chinking of one tone. Logs with the bark removed will weather to soft grays and browns, but if a definite tone of brown, gray, or green is preferred it can be applied with the wood oil, which acts as a preservative as

The Craftsman Farm is now restored and open for visits during the summer. Contact:

The Craftsman Farm Foundation
2353 Route 10
Morris Plains, NJ
07950
(973) 540-1165

well as medium for the stain.

Log houses properly built upon stone or concrete foundations will last from generation to generation—a constant delight to the eye and source of satisfaction in every way.

In the early days a woodsman generally built his house of logs without removing the bark, not because he thought it looked better, or that it blended in an inconspicuous way with is surroundings, but because he was usually in haste to occupy his home. And the little house, not much better than a hut, was never intended to endure a century or more, though such log houses have occasionally stood the test of time for more than the three-score-years-and-ten allotted to man's term of usefulness. These primitive houses were pointed with whatever mud or clay was nearest at hand, and, needless to say, the task of rechinking was of frequent occurrence; but if the foundation be well laid, the logs well seasoned, the chinking well done with cement mortar, the log house of today will hold its own among ancestral homes of the future.

Logs of chestnut with the bark removed have great substantial value in building these houses. They weather beautifully or take any stain desired. In the absence of chestnut, cedar logs could be used; these are rich in tone without the necessity of applying a stain. Oak logs have also proved satisfactory.

**T**here have been successive mini-waves of this type of camp near ski resorts in Aspen, Telluride, and Tahoe, near lakes in North Carolina, Vermont, Maine, New Hampshire, Michigan, and many other places. Two such places, the Smith Family Lodge in Warren, Vermont, and Atkins Lodge in Killington, Vermont, were designed by David Sellers. He follows a similar philosophy to that of William West Durant in that he incorporates natural materials from the land into the body of the structures he is designing.

Twelve hundred dollars can build a 24' x 32' log cabin from scratch.

National Parks Go Rustic

**A**t the turn of the twentieth century, the National Park Service adopted rustic—really a Durant rustic—as its official style. They built colossal structures—like Old Faithful Inn in 1904 and other work by the Civilian Conservation Corps (CCC) during the depression—rustic cabins, and pavilions all over state and national parks. Timberline Lodge on Mt. Hood in Oregon is a stellar example. As a result, there were ever-increasing numbers of visitors to the parks who saw and associated rustic architecture with the forest and nature itself.

©38432G—OLD FAITHFUL INN, YELLOWSTONE NATIONAL PARK

ZEMAN, MONTANA

Camp-Inspired Rustic Work

Although much of the log-home movement has been shaped with aesthetics worked out in the detailing of the early great camps, a great deal of the furniture work supporting rustic builders in the last twenty years has sprouted from the idiosyncrasies found in the great camps.

65

Other "Great" Camps

Though the wealthy may have been trendsetters and self-interested patrons, it was the rest of America who embraced the spirit of the camp—that moment away from normal life when certain bruises of the heart and soul get time to mend. It may be the vacation home or the weekend getaway, but it's a recognized and needed antidote.

As mentioned earlier, there seems to be a movement back to the woods after violent national traumas. There is the need for what could only be called repose. It often appears in even the most private of family albums. This one was assembled just after World War I. It is the work, or play, of a man quite proud of his family and his camp, Weomah.

Another Camp . . . in Quebec

Every summer for more than thirty years, the Saltonstall family drove ten hours from home in New Hampshire to a lake in Quebec. After two boat rides and a forty-five-minute hike with all the provisions, they arrived at their getaway.

Aurora Foods, owners of Log Cabin Maple Syrup, donated one million dollars to fix up four hundred log cabins in the National Park System. Aurora Foods has redesigned their plastic Log Cabin Syrup bottle in the shape of a cabin to create awareness and hopefully generate money for the preservation of log cabins.

Cabins Without Photos

Sometimes the cabins disappear, but the memories do not. A woman from the Bronx shares this memory:

⊱ ⊱ ⊱

I've few memories of my youth, but one that has remained with me for almost forty years was an afternoon spent in a log cabin. I was in high school in the Bronx and had a friend who, one weekend, invited me to go along with her and her parents for a day-trip. We drove somewhere north of New York City to visit their friend, who was the headmaster at what was then referred to as a "reform school" for boys. Adjacent to the school, nestled in a wooded area, was the headmaster's home . . . a log cabin. Although it was spring, it had begun to rain and the dampness crept into my bones and made me yearn for a hot drink and warm sweater. The cabin we entered was small, and the golden patina of its wood and curving repetitive pattern of its walls made me feel as though I was being enveloped in a warm embrace. There on the beds were genuine bear rugs creating a sense of having moved backward to another century. I can still hear the rain splattering on the leaves outside as we remained safely wrapped in a cocoon of myriad textures. From the imagination of my teen girlhood to even my present adult self, it seemed to me that that space was infused with a sensuality that became etched in my mind as the quintessential setting for a romantic interlude.

DAN MEETS BR'ER FISH NEAR A LOG CABIN

For a summer in 1976, I rented a log cabin in rural Pennsylvania. It was built in the 1920s and was crisp and clean and comfortable.

What I remember most is how dark it was and how it immediately made me feel that I was just visiting; that other people, other spirits had draw on the place: the current owners, the original builder. But there was something even more about this cabin. It was situated on a little piece of land with a stream in the back and a brook in the front. It wasn't really an island; it was a pretend island. There were trout in the stream in the back, and I was a fisherman at that time. I had just decided to keep only the fish I could make into a meal that day. If I caught too few, I would release them all. Four trout were what I was fishing for. To keep the first few, I decided to get a big spaghetti pot, submerge it in the stream, and put the trout in the pot with a grate on the top of the pot, weighted by a rock. Great idea.

Well, I caught an eleven-inch trout and carefully placed it in the holding pot and put the grate on top and went upstream to keep fishing. When I returned a half hour later, with a few more fish, there was the first one waiting for me. He was swimming in circles around the OUTSIDE of the spaghetti pot. The rock was in place, the grate was in place.

I was sure I heard the bubbly sound of fish laughing. I let the other ones go and just stood there as they started some fish story between themselves:

"So I says to him, 'Oh, please Mr. Dan, do anything to me, gut me now, filet me and fry me, but whatever you do don't put me in that cold water. And please don't put me in a pot with a grate on top'."

THE MORPHING OF THE LOG CABIN

As the frontier of land closed at the turn of the twentieth century, the log cabin started a metamorphosis. It had never really stayed the same in the 250 years it had been on the American continent. The original style of the Finns had been tweaked, souped up, and customized by every single group and every single individual who tried their hands at it.

There would always be handcrafted cabins built by individuals and groups pioneering into new lands, particularly in the Canadian West, but it was not with the thrust that the previous two centuries had known.

The Image of the Log Cabin

One new form of the log cabin that appeared had begun about fifty years prior. It was the *reference* to the log cabin or the *image* of the log cabin. Invoking the humble cabin was an important political strategy. William Henry Harrison, in 1852, used the log cabin as his campaign icon. He had *not* been born in a log cabin, but owned a piece of property in Illinois where a log cabin stood. Even then, the deep nostalgic quality of the cabin was evident. He won.

But after the land rush was over, by about 1890, the log-cabin style was being absorbed into structures in national parks, shelters along the Appalachian Trail, tourist cabins, grand lodges, taverns (who hasn't been to an Old Log Inn?), and roadside stands.

It became the symbol of vacation homes and destinations of vacations as it was enshrined in theme parks like Frontier Lands, Cowboy Villages, and ultimately in Disneyland and DisneyWorld.

Many of the captains of industry were the ones who first assembled the collections and recollections of the past in the form of Williamsburg, Winterthur, and Deerfield Village, and it was their great camps that set the standard for vacations.

How many references to log cabins or the log-cabin icon can you think of? Write them down and compare them with those of your friends.

THE UNIQUE LOG HOUSE, A RIPLEY "BELIEVE IT OR NOT," CONSTRUCTED OF CROSS CUT REDWOOD LOGS

71

TO O

One reason the log cabin was so well suited to America was that it needed very few tools for construction. Actually, one tool could get it done: the ax. In a raw new country, especially on the frontier, people often had to rely on what they already owned and brought with them.

The ax was used in a very careful and exact manner for many tasks, from felling trees to making furniture.

Even as a furniture maker today, I use the same techniques in a certain style of chair.

Many people who build log cabins learn that tools are one of the ways people engage in a very old practice: the need to shape-shift. In some places it is believed that people can change their form of being and become wind, birds, or water. Cultures with shamans believe in this. The writings of Carlos Castaneda have helped understand this better. It was a part of ancient cultures—cultures that are old but perhaps not gone. The Celts took shape-shifting as a fact of life.

I agree that this is a strange occurrence. But that is not to say the human need to shape-shift hasn't taken on other expressions. Certainly, any medium we

L S

The point is that the trickster, whom we will call "old pioneer," can make a house from the trees. His methods include first his attitude toward the world. It's a "can-do, we'll-work-it out" world-view, and his helpers are his tools: his ax, his auger, and his knife.

The need to shape-shift persists and has found one way, among many, to be met through tools, workshops, and projects. When we pick up a tool, our hand grasps it; our sweat is absorbed into the tool handle, and we absorb some of the sweat left for us by others. We have begun to shift our shape. Then we apply our hand and tool, our head and heart, to our project. Materials change from one way to another. Time passes in a way unlike other times. All of a sudden it's late or early and we put down the tools and return to our regular world. This seems so simple and common. It is and it isn't. We may not become the boar or the bird, but we have become the saw, the rasp, the

work with changes us; we are never quite the same. Marshall McLuhan spent most of his life working on his theory that every extension of man has a profound effect on who man sees himself to be and, indeed, who he actually is. In *The Trickster Makes the World,* Lewis Hyde presents the idea that shape-shifting is quite alive and well in the form of the trickster, he who violates the good order of things. The trickster shows that the way things—material things, institutions, everything—are put together is not permanent. The shape of the world can change. To put this in a very positive way, the trickster is able to work with whatever happens; he can work with contingencies; he can improvise.

73

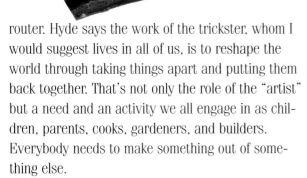

router. Hyde says the work of the trickster, whom I would suggest lives in all of us, is to reshape the world through taking things apart and putting them back together. That's not only the role of the "artist" but a need and an activity we all engage in as children, parents, cooks, gardeners, and builders. Everybody needs to make something out of something else.

One of the great things about the magic of using tools is that you don't have to build something as big as a log cabin in order to gain from the experience. You can build something as simple as a twig picture frame or a towel rack.

There is such gravity to doing a project; sometimes it seems like a project just to begin. I've been practicing small, modest activities. They are exercises in materials, tools, speed, imagination, and play. I want simple tools, ones that fit in a pocket or a small satchel. I want materials that are already here. So many people make a project of just getting the tools and materials. They never get to the making part! They grumble that "If only I had wood as big or as dry or as interesting, and if I only had the right tools, then, boy oh boy, could I make something."

Sometimes I find a branch that has fallen out of a tree, a black walnut shell discarded by a squirrel, or a pile of cut-backs from one of my shrubs. I use these as the givens of my project: "Here it is, perfectly imperfect! What can I do? No whining now; no ifs, onlys, or buts. What can I do?"

Often the whining comes from a certain kind of unease, a discomfort with what other people might say. There's an easy way around this: don't make the object for yourself. Forget you and think of making a gift for somebody else. It immediately frees you to enjoy spontaneity and playfulness. Even if it could possibly be seen as a dumb, ill-proportioned, ill-crafted item, the fact that it is a gift outshines everything else. You will welcome the following responses: "What! For me? Why I'm, I'm . . . It's so unusual. Oh, thank you."

And then again, it might just be beautiful and inventive. You never know till you try, and if it isn't your best project, maybe the next one will be.

Tools the pioneers wished they'd had:

Short Kutt Saw—A flexible saw made of something like a chainsaw blade. You use two hands and cut very fast. It collapses into a little pouch.

Survival Cards—Three different decks of cards with the numbers and suits containing information on emergency care, and edible and poisonous plants and wild foods.

Folding Buck Saw— Everything comes in a tube and assembles quickly.

Source: Brigade Quartermasters 1-800-338-4327

How to Make a Log Cabin Picture Frame in an Hour or More (or Less)

Step 1: Get a picture you want to frame: a photo, drawing, or magazine picture.

Step 2: Find or cut a stiff backing, such as a piece of quarter-inch plywood, a cigar-box top, or parts of a fruit box.

Step 3: Make this backing about an inch bigger all around than your picture.

Step 4: Mount the picture on the stiff backing using glue or spray adhesive.

Step 5: Get some sticks that are freshly cut or even tree-dropped.

Step 6: Begin to arrange the sticks around your picture. Are you going to be neat or are you a jumbler? Do you like them as flat as possible or are you building them up? Keep arranging.

Step 7: Soon you will have a few parts of the arrangement that keep reappearing. You like them. That's pleasing. You are developing a style. Keep going till you meet the Critic.*

Step 8: After the Critic is comfortably seated, get back to work and attach those sticks to the board around your picture. There are so many ways: hot glue, drilling little holes and sewing the sticks on with thread or fine wire, putting a squeeze of construction adhesive in that one-inch border and squishing the sticks into it, nailing, or tying or lashing all the sticks together with wire or cord.

After it is done and dried, consider painting it. WHAT? You say you would like to try another with pieces of broken dishes or small stones? Good for you!

*The Critic is a Frankenstein-like character made up of bits and pieces of all the people you can remember (and some you have seemed to forget) who gave you that uneasy feeling that you weren't quite good enough. When the Critic visits (and she does!), make room for her. Invite her to stay, but put her over to the side where she can mumble and clear her throat and roll her eyes and you can learn not to pay attention. You can keep on with your work. The two of you—you and the person receiving the gift—are stronger than the Critic.

TREES ... WITH AN INTERRUPTION

For the Iroquois and other Native Americans, there was a keen awareness of the sacredness of all life. Each animal, each tree, the water, the air, and earth had soul.

🐦 🐦 🐦

The ancient Celts had similar beliefs, and almost every culture reveres the tree and attributes integrity and life force to both the living and inanimate worlds. That perception, as an active part of daily life, is more remote from us today. But there are traces even in our ways. Don't we speak of our family tree, the Tree of Knowledge? Aren't tree-lined streets more beautiful and tree-filled properties more valuable? It is possible to experience and appreciate the belief that the world is ensouled, and we are just a part of it.

From trees we get food, medicine, shelter, fuel, and the raw materials for our art and craft and culture-making: wood, lumber, paper. But more importantly, from trees we can learn about beauty, grace, and movement. Trees are stable and long-living. Trees make us feel small and protected.

"The Chandalier Tree" at Underwood Park on Redwood Highway.

ABOUT BARK, BUGS, AND FAERIES

Tree Project

Select a tree you see every day. Look at it a little longer than you normally do.

How tall is it? What does its shape look like? Draw it.

How different does it look from different angles or at different times of the day?

What else happens in and around this tree? Keep a few notes.

Close your eyes and feel the tree. Leave your hands on the tree for a minute. **Congratulations!** You have just started reclaiming your right to experience the sacredness of all life.

The trees will continue to help you as long as you spend time with them.

16 John S. Haller and his rustic chair made from wood from Valley Forge. *L.D. Miller, Publisher* Rutherford, Pa.

Trees are, literally, the core of the log-cabin experience. When people choose to work with logs for a home, they are making a very complicated and profound statement about themselves, their values, and their sense of their own future. It is usually rooted in the past—past experiences with trees and the forest. The forests have always marked the edge of civilization. When you are in the forest, the rules of good order may not apply. For a few years, I called one of my rustic studios *FORIS*, a term from the Middle Ages referring to treed areas outside the control of governing institutions. It was home to outcasts, visionaries, misfits, and saints. It was the place the noble knight went wild. It was the abode of chaos, not exactly disorder, but an alternative order that challenged prevailing order.

The trees, whether as lurching chairs or looming beams and columns, embody and exude that disturbing chaos of the forest. Some people like it. They want to be near it and feel it. It has a timeless quality.

Bark

There is something very special about bark. Like so many parts of the tree, it is closely associated with the human body. The bark is the skin. It became the protective covering of the sides and the roof of Native American and early pioneer shelters, thus being something people got under and were protected by. But it was also kindling for fires and the stuff of tying and lashing and the source of beverages and chemicals, such as tannin for leather.

Today bark carries the legacy of what it was; the enduring charm of the white birch baskets speaks to this. There are many basket makers and artists who work with bark. Some use traditional methods of weaving and veneering; others knit with it, chew it, or "paint" with small, mosaic-size pieces. I still use hickory bark as a seating material. I get it from Brian

Collecting Fresh Bark Kills a Tree

It is often thought that you can remove bark from a living tree and it will not harm the tree. However, such a traumatic event usually weakens the tree so much that it eventually becomes infected and dies. A person who works with bark needs to understand this role in the stream of life. Yes, he's responsible for the tree's death, but being alive is a fundamentally aggressive act. There is a quote that says nature is less about death than about transformation. So, as living, active aggressors we are a part—only a part—of the transformation of materials.

We are most alive when we are creatively engaged with the world around us. That means making, doing, arranging.

Boggs, my friend and a chair maker in Kentucky. Bark is still harvested in late spring when the trees are filled with sap and have just started to leaf out. It is a long and careful task. The bark can be harvested and then dried and soaked again when it's time to use it.

> *"Nature does not complete things. She is chaotic. Man must finish, and he does so by making a garden and building a wall."*
>
> **—ROBERT FROST**

Bark-Veneered Room by Jerry Farrell, 1991

About sixty medium-sized white birches were harvested from the top of a quarry in order to make a 12' x 15' room. The bark was immediately stapled to pieces of plywood and stacked and skidded down a small mountain. It was air-dried for about eight weeks, during which time it shrunk and pulled off the staples. It was then glued with carpenter's glue to pieces of plywood that had already been fitted to the walls of the room. The plywood panels were then screwed to the walls and the seams were covered with half-round strips of moose-maple sapling that had first been kiln-dried and split on a table saw.

BUGS

Bugs are the keepers of time in the forest. Sometimes I think the bugs own the forest. They know when and how to appear and disappear. They know about light, the length of days, and minute changes in temperature and humidity. They know how to take care of business and get on with offspring. Bugs alarm people because of their wiliness.

Much of my life with bugs has been trying to convince people there are *not* bugs in the rustic furniture they have just gotten. I started collecting the odd visitor or two or twelve that showed up. I kept them in jars and boxes until some little mite or other bug buried deep within *them* ate them all to dust. So much for my collection. Bugs help me understand that life is in motion.

A very popular question in the log-cabin world is the bug question. In literature, in discussions, and on several internet forums, there is abiding concern about unseen bugs who may be lurking in new logs, old logs, all logs. It is a way of recognizing those timekeepers.

Those Frass Makers
(Apologies and respect to Mason Williams)

Those wood beetles, they sure do like wood.
Chompin' on the bark and suckin' on the sap,
chewing on the woodyparts and laying them eggs.
Then time goes by
and squishy little wormy bugs
wake up and start chewin' on the woodyparts.
I swear, I truly swear I can hear them
making that frass,
such soft fine powdery frass!
And then they chew their way out
into air and light and more space
than they could ever imagine.
A new world
Hey! Other Bugs!
who smell different,
good different.
And so it starts again,
those wood beetles
they sure do.

Bug Watching

I am sitting in a room in the middle of February and every day half a dozen ladybugs appear from somewhere and clack around on the blinds and then dry up. I've tried taking them down to a plant that has aphids, but they just crawl off and spend their time looking out the window. There seem to be different back designs. What do your bugs look like? Make some drawings.

83

From *Walden*, Thoreau's ode to bugs, from 1854, placed importantly in the last few paragraphs:

> *Everyone has heard the story which has gone the rounds of New England, of a strong and beautiful bug which came out of the dry leaf of an old table of apple-tree wood, which had stood in a farmer's kitchen for sixty years, first in Connecticut, and afterward in Massachusetts—from an egg deposited in the living tree many years earlier still, as appeared by counting the annual layers beyond it; which has heard gnawing out for several weeks, hatched perchance by the heat of an urn. Who does not feel his faith in a resurrection and immortality strengthened by hearing of this? Who knows what beautiful and winged life, whose egg has been buried for ages under many concentric layers of woodenness in the dead dry life of society, deposited at first in the alburnum of the green and living tree, which has been gradually converted into the semblance of its well-seasoned tomb—heard per-chance gnawing out now for years by the astonished family of man, as they sat round the festive board—may unexpectedly come forth from amidst society's most trivial and handselled furniture, to enjoy its perfect sum-mer life at last!*

These hand-tinted pictures are from Thoreau's time.

Tree Time

Time seems to keep appearing as a theme. Take time to watch a tree through the seasons. As trees change, they are the same . . . or are they?

Up the Tree: The Nest

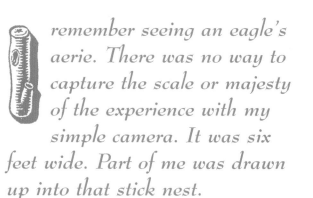

I remember seeing an eagle's aerie. There was no way to capture the scale or majesty of the experience with my simple camera. It was six feet wide. Part of me was drawn up into that stick nest.

There I am crouching in the bottom of the nest, waiting for the adult birds to come back, hoping they wouldn't notice my human form . . . hoping they would feed me. Another part of me, my rabbit-self, wanted to flee, knowing I had gotten much too close for my own safety.

A few years later, I was fortunate enough to watch a pair of osprey in their big, but not eagle-roomy, nest. They just looked down on me, pitiful as I was, stuck on the ground.

Artist Patrick Dougherty of North Carolina travels the country giving earthbound humans the thrill of the nest. Here, young Eliza Mack has just emerged from a Dougherty installation at the Katonah Museum in 1989.

TREEH

Treehouses are man's way to try to better himself, to rise above his earthbound station. People have climbed up the trees ever since they climbed down.

OUSES

Down the Tree:  aeries

*A*nother element of time rooted in the trees is the unseen . . . down in the earth among the roots. That is said to be the home of the faeries, elves, and dryads.

Faeries

Come away, O human child!
to the waters and the wild
with a faery, hand in hand,
for the world's more full of weeping
than you can understand . . .

—W. B. YEATS

Faeries are not a well-known part of the American experience. But they have long been associated with the woods and forests, which is just about all this continent was a few hundred years ago. Learning how to recognize them takes practice. Most of what we know comes from the British Isles. There are many different kinds of faeries: benign and ill-tempered, ugly and pleasing. They share certain characteristics humans have difficulty with. They have an ability to shift time and shapes. They embody the unpredictability of the forest. They can catch you and vex you.

Perhaps here in America they are not quite as pixie-like as they are elsewhere. Washington Irving's story about Rip Van Winkle is really about a man caught by faeries, mountain folk, perhaps the spirits of Henry Hudson's crew, who put the twenty-year sleep on him. Rip was caught in the Catskill Glen, not too far from where I sit. Contact with faeries is about altered time and shape when you grow old or stay young.

Dwelling on faeries in a book on log cabins is necessary because, *come on*, nobody really needs the heartache and headache of a log cabin. The cost, the upkeep . . . and all those logs! Behind every log-cabin owner is a faery, reaching up from another place to make him think a log cabin is a very fine, efficient, sensible form of housing. *Indeed!* Even if that is true, and it might be, there is something more overpowering about the symbol of the tree and the log and the dream. In the quiet moments away from the mortgage and taxes and daily details, there are those images imagined or from the magazines where the glow of

the cabin, inside and out, is radiant, like amber or maple syrup. There is something timeless, almost heavenly, about the beckoning image of the log cabin.

Today we sidle up to the faery world on certain holidays: St. Patrick's Day is marked by shifting shapes. People dress in costumes and march up and down streets; they drink more than the usual amount of intoxicants, thereby ensuring certain contact with spirits. Their return to the regular world the next day may be difficult, marked by a lateness, an inability to focus on mundane tasks, and the need to tell stories of what happened to them. This is all the stuff of

faeries. The same can be written of Mardi Gras celebration on Shrove Tuesday, Halloween, and New Year's Eve. It happens on birthdays, anniversaries, and before weddings. In this way, faeries are the guides to and denizens of altered realities.

Cats are one way of contacting faeries. Various spells call upon the ways of the cat, and if you think about it, the way they look, stare, sit, and squint reflects a self-assured, knowledgeable quality. Cats know something. Like faeries, they have a sense of altered time. They are witnesses for the defense in a world of schedules, coffee, and alarm clocks. And, if you pay attention, you will notice that cats practice a form of meditation, beginning with crossing their toes and closing their eyes.

Keep in mind that this is all coming from a person who did not like cats at all until summer solstice three years ago when a small stray cat arrived at my house and decided to make it home. She is now bigger, and I have spent much time watching and learning from her about time and movement . . . and specks of dust in the sun.

The enduring story of Peter Pan is a tale from and about faeries. It is about arrested and altered perceptions. Peter and his boys live beneath the trees, in kind of a natural log cabin in Neverland, which resembles the ancient Celtic Otherworld of the Sidhe alluded to by Yeats in the poem fragment on page 90.

"I like trees because they seem more resigned to the way they have to live than other things do."

—WILLA CATHER

Perhaps faeries are the reason we feel something for trees. Even when we are bending a branch, breaking off a leaf, or even chainsawing one down, there is a connection. We feel an even stronger connection when we plant trees or care for our trees. In J.R.R. Tolkien's famous *Lord of the Rings*, the trees were taken care of by the Ents, tree-shepherds. They share the tree-like qualities of steadiness, focus "and they are better at getting inside things." That may mean a kind of ability to understand and empathize, to be a quiet listener. Isn't that exactly what happens when we go to the forest and sit beneath a tree? Don't we calm down? Even when we step into a log cabin, isn't that first moment one of quiet?

In 1990, twenty American carpenters were brought to Japan to assemble cabins because Japanese couldn't keep up with the supply and demand.

"If you are thinking a year ahead, sow a seed. If you are thinking ten years ahead, plant a tree. If you are thinking one hundred years ahead, educate the people."

—**CHINESE POET, 500 B.C.**

MABEL LUCIE ATTWELL

The Ents today have addresses, phones, e-mails, and Websites. Here are three different kinds. There are many more in the resource section.

Plant-It 2000

A nonprofit foundation dedicated to properly planting, maintaining, and protecting as many indigenous trees as possible worldwide.

9457 South University Boulevard, Suite 310
Highlands Ranch, Colorado 80126
voice: (303) 221-0077
fax: (303) 221-0090

email:plantit@tesser.com
http://www.tesser.com/plantit/

The American Association of Amateur Arborists

A loose association of individuals and groups who are interested in learning and sharing more about trees and other woody plants. They encourage members to take tree walks and make a tree map of their own area, listing at least fifty different trees. This group of Ents is truly magical. The only way to reach them is through the internet.

http://www.arborworks.org

Swan View Coalition

An activist group that has developed a "Code of Forest Ethics" that makes the restoration of damaged watersheds and forest ecosystems via road obliteration top priority.

3165 Foothill Road
Kalispell, Montana 59901
(406) 755-1379

email: redraven@digisys.net
http://www.wildrockies.org/Talus/Campaign/ForEthix.html

"A thing is right when it tends to preserve the integrity, stability, and beauty of the biotic community. It is wrong when it tends otherwise."

—ALDO LEOPOLD

The Code of Forest Ethics

The greatest threats to forest ecosystems are too many roads, clearcuts, and damaged watersheds, not too many trees.

These problems are a result of logging and road building, not the suppression of wildfire.

We subscribe to these principles:

All remaining roadless and unlogged areas must be preserved. The continued march into increasingly scarce native forest does not promote sustainability.

Watersheds which are below standards for water quality, fisheries, wildlife habitat and wildlife security must be brought up to all standards before further timber sales are contemplated.

Road obliteration and reclamation are the primary and most cost-effective ways to accomplish watershed recovery, protect fish and wildlife habitat, and reestablish wildlife security.

Ecosystem restoration is a goal and process worthy of public investment. It also provides meaningful, well-paying jobs.

Timber sales neither provide reliable funds for restoration work nor duplicate the natural role of wildfire. They shall not be promoted for such purposes.

Forest stewardship must be viewed and practiced as more than a kinder and gentler form of tree farming. In already damaged areas, it must begin with ecosystem restoration.

It must also recognize the essential role that dead trees play in the forest ecosystem.

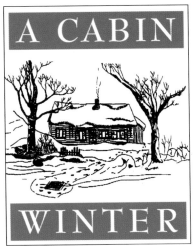

A CABIN WINTER

I learned to respect the Adirondack winter because of a series of events. The first incident occurred when I opened my eyes after a night's sleep. My head was stuck to the pillow—my hair had frozen to the frost on the cabin wall. Frosted walls are a feature of life in the far north. A layer of ice a quarter of an inch thick covers the walls most of the winter, brought about by intense cold, uninsulated buildings, and potbelly heat. My side of the bed was against the wall, and this morning I was literally stuck to the wallboards. Luckily, a haircut solved the problem.

Another morning I awoke and felt a layer of frost on my upper lip and under my nose. I saw my breath as white smoke, and I knew the stove had gone out during the night. I put my slipper socks over my thermal underwear and went to the stove, stirred the coals, heaved in a few pieces of beech, and dove back under the covers. Hearing the crackle of the wood as it flamed became my security signal on cold winter mornings.

—LINDA RUNYON

Linda Runyon, known as the wild food lady, began wild food experiments by living off the land back in 1972. For thirteen years she made her home in a cabin in the Adirondacks. Her most recent book, *From Crabgrass Muffins to Pine Needle Tea,* can be found at her Web site, www.wild-food.org.

TIME

ime is another of the great invisibles connected to the log cabin. If you're building a log cabin, you know well the time, or "times," involved. There is the time of conception and dreaming about the log home that could go on for years through several cities and various jobs with children coming and going. In this time, the log cabin is *already* there for you, offering something stable and steady in an otherwise changing world. You can build and rebuild the home as often as you want. On the other hand, if you had been a pioneer, you would have started and finished your log cabin within a week. The very first night you would have made a half-face camp or lean-to. Time for pioneers was not for dreaming.

Next there is the research time, the time when you start looking for the right property, materials, and instruction or a contractor. This is a real time activity, bound in the details of the marketplace. It involves banks, suppliers, and truckers. This is the time when the log home becomes *this* log home. It's a time of weighing, judging, making decisions, and waiting. It is a long time: five or even ten years or more.

But this isn't the most important form of time. The log cabin, in mind, heart, or on a piece of earth, has a way of transporting a person to another time. It could be a time from memory with a father or mother or friend; it could be a time from deeper memory of a sense of belonging. This is the lingering metaphorical

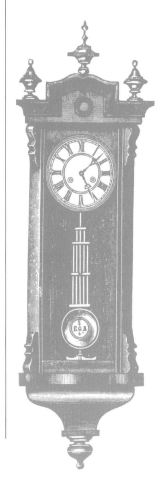

importance of the log cabin.

I think it was the altered sense of time possessed by the log cabin people that so struck the travelers and visitors. These people didn't live by the same time. Life wasn't necessarily slower, but the rhythms were different and more varied. They were tied to weather, animals, and earth. That varied sense of time makes being alive most rewarding. It offers the chance and opportunity to wander and to lose track of time but not disappear. A comforting bumper sticker quotes J.R.R. Tolkien from *The Lord of the Rings*: "All who wander are not lost."

For those of us who will never build or even visit one, the log cabin is the reminder of altered time. There are many ways to change our experience of time: gardening, building projects, meditation, reading, and one of my new favorites, writing Haiku poetry. I sort of knew what Haiku was, but I never really tried it until recently at the guidance of poet Clark Strand, who has written two very inviting books— *Seeds from the Birch Tree: Writing Haiku and the Spiritual Journey* and *The Wooden Bowl: Simple Meditation for Everyday Life.* Both are published by Hyperion Books.

Haiku, very simply, is minimal-structure, maximum-impact poetry rooted in nature and the present moment. The goal is the haiku moment . . . that blink-wince-flash where you see and understand something differently than just the moment before. The poem is just the tool, the conduit of your own insight. It can be done with no tools, anywhere, anytime.

Haiku is three lines,
just seventeen syllables,
no rhymes required.

The first line has five syllables, the second seven, and the third five. Count these on your fingers.

There is a reference to nature, the present season, and the last line often recasts the meaning of the first two in order to provoke the impact of the poem, thus creating the haiku moment.

I am finishing up this book in the month of March when there is a change in the weather—snow then warmth, lots of mud, and ladybugs on the windows. That is the stuff used to write the following haiku. Here are a few from twenty minutes of finger-counting:

If you did get out
and felt the mud, snow, brisk air
would you come back in?

The bare trees seem dead
but the dirvish of dry leaves
foretells renewal.

Making Haiku

Try one!

Start with the same natural element, the tree. Be quiet and observe a tree. Start counting your syllables; five, seven, and five. Share it with your friends and family or send it to a random list of e-mail recipients. Challenge them to do the same.

GHOSTS

Ghosts are harder to see than bugs. By ghosts I mean the felt presence of the past. We live in the moment, but there are millions of moments that have preceded and helped form our moment, and, in a way, they are present and can be felt. Some people are better tuned to feeling the presence of the past than others, but, nonetheless, it affects us all.

Ghosts of the Land

From the rock and earth itself there are messages. Some places "feel" better than others. Before we bought all this land, the Native Americans were here and had quite a different relationship. The Lenni Lenape, part of the Delaware tribe, are in the land I live on. I can't say I get postcards, but I do have a sense that I am only a steward of this land. Despite my deed, my title insurance, and my property markers, I am just passing through. Almost every time I go into my yard I feel that.

The Ghosts of Structures and Things

The materials of our homes, furniture, and objects carry ghosts. Other people have touched these things. They have made decisions about them and moved them about. There is a part of them on those things, and it can't help but get on us. That's the attraction of old tools, barnwood, driftwood, and old broken furniture. The ghosts come out easier and faster than with new stuff.

The Ghosts of the Trees

One great thing the log cabin has going is the ghost of the tree. In honoring the log by not turning it into lumber, the tree continues to emanate *prana*, life energy. Trees are here to move along the life energy of the world. They gather it in the branches and roots and pass it along to other beings. That's one reason people just like log cabins. People can feel the energy.

Ruins, like the old farm equipment in my neighbors' pastures, show us that something remains of beauty when its function has departed. Soul is then revealed, as though it had been hidden for years under well-oiled functioning. Soul is not about function, it is about beauty, form and memory.

—THOMAS MOORE, *THE CARE OF THE SOUL*

Family Ghosts

No matter how much we think we are the acme of civilization, it isn't true. We are just the next version of what goes on. There is a wealth of information and wisdom in our own families. Our edge or advantage is that we are the ones who are alive and able to shuffle and shift and wring some meaning out of the centuries of people before us.

Ethnicity and Family Stories

We all came from somewhere. There is stock in us. The older I get, the more I look like my father and like a lot of other Irish American men. (Actually, years ago, I probably looked like a lot of other Irish American young men.) My point here is that there is a lot to gain by understanding more about what we share, not just as Americans, but what is shared by being part of an ethnic group. Contrary to what you may have heard, all ethnicity didn't melt when it hit the shores of America. Although this focuses on the Irish American experience, the approach is the same for any ethnic group.

Contemporary literature of Irish Americans, notably Mary Gordon and Frank McCourt, touches all of us. There are histories and educational and psychological textbooks on the subtle and not-so-subtle differences between American ethnic groups. I'm fourth-generation American Irish and German, but I swear I share attitudes and dispositions described as Irish or German.

In describing the Irish, Sean O'Faolin describes the ancient Irish as if they were the American pioneers by saying they loved being under the open sky in the country. They built few roads and buildings, and enjoyed vast woodlands.

I spend this time on the Irish for more than personal reasons. They greatly swelled the numbers of the people pioneering, and the attitudes that came with them became the prevailing winds of frontier pioneer life.

This relates to log cabins because as each ethnic group saw and learned about log cabins from the Swedes or Finns, they made changes in the cabin. These changes sprouted from their own backgrounds, the real experiences of housing elsewhere, and something deeper—an attitude toward home, place, and family that was as inherited as hair color, eyes, nose, and other features. The more we can learn about who our relatives were and how they saw the world, the better our chance of knowing who *we* are.

Most of us know something about particular relatives, even if it is a sentence, a place, or a photo.

This is the place to start dreaming and feeling your way back into your own murky past. While working on this book, I remembered a family history I compiled about thirty-five years ago when I was in high school where I called old relatives and wrote down their family recollections. I remembered that there had been a log cabin in my family past. Yes, Michael Fuery, an Irish emigrant, dug the Erie Canal and built a log cabin near there. I spent time thinking about this man, my great-great-grandfather.

To my great-great-grandfather, Michael Fuery, who built a log cabin in Johnson Creek, New York, around 1845:

Michael Fuery,
Why did you leave County Roscommon?
Was it the Famine?
Did you sing in church in America, too?

Michael Fuery,
What part of the Erie Canal did you dig?
When did you build that log cabin in Johnson Creek?
How big was it? Were you proud?

Michael Fuery, at 32, you got married
What was she like, that Ann Fox, at 15?

What did she look like? Smell like?
Was she beautiful? Tell me!
Were there looks between you?
Did you love Ann Fox when she was old?

My daughter, your great-great-great-grand-daughter,
is now 15.
I don't think she'll have nine children.

I've never seen your picture.
How long did you live?
What did you think about
when you were old?

Michael Fuery,
Did your children take care of you?
Were you a bitter man?
Did your cabin burn down?

I'm going to try to find
what parts of you are
still lingering.

I'll write again,
Michael Fuery.

I began calling very distant relatives. These were people who no one in living memory had ever contacted—third and fourth cousins twice removed. It was a little silly but then I began to feel more connected. We were all telling each other job stories, children stories, and extracting promises to come visit. We were all variations from that man Michael and that wife Ann. What was happening was kin or clan, quite unusual in twenty-first-century America! I don't know if anyone in my family lives in a log cabin or has built one recently, but one log cabin a long time ago has started a buzz within parts of a family.

For me it was pretty straightforward. All parts of my family, both Irish and German, came from Europe and settled and stayed in the same sixty-mile area around Lake Ontario. But many, probably most, Americans are the product of pioneer families who moved continually and might count five or six different ethnic backgrounds per family.

Nonetheless diluted, like homeopathy, the power of ethnicity is still there.

Contact a Great-Great-Ancestor

Try one!

If you don't have a name, you may have a photo; if you don't have either, look in the mirror.

Ask your nameless, photo-less relative about that nose, those ears, lips, and cheeks.

Ask about the concerns you have (perhaps they are not just yours).

Be direct in your questions. Wait for the next questions or perhaps some answers. Try it.

PLAYING/MAKING

laying/making is a basic human need. It involves selecting materials and organizing the manner of building. The process helps to repair and restore us; thus, good making remakes the maker.

Making is really the act of making something special. When we make, we immerse ourselves in time and space and material and make decisions about arrangement, shape, textures, time. Making requires that we engage on four different but related levels of experience at once: Making is a statement about our culture, what we know and value, what we have absorbed and emanate about our collective life. Making is about our self, our body and spirit, and it illustrates how brave and adventurous we are. It is also about our lone voice. Most common today, making is about a product. (You made that!) The product is the externalization of the process.

Making is also a series of very subtle, elusive, vanishing, meandering but powerful processes. There are decisions, attitudes, changes, moods, emanations, flushes, fatigues, elations, frustrations, and feelings of fullness and emptiness, tightness and

lightness. The process is not as easily talked about or written about as the product. It cannot be quantified quite as easily but it is nonetheless powerful.

One way to understand more about making is to just call it "play" and excuse yourself for a while to go play. That play might be a project, game, recipe, or poem.

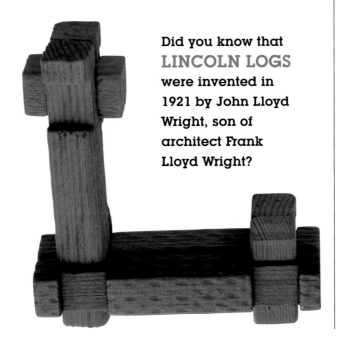

Did you know that LINCOLN LOGS were invented in 1921 by John Lloyd Wright, son of architect Frank Lloyd Wright?

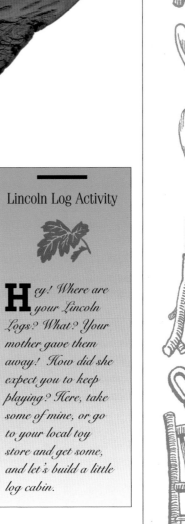

Lincoln Log Activity

Hey! Where are your Lincoln Logs? What? Your mother gave them away! How did she expect you to keep playing? Here, take some of mine, or go to your local toy store and get some, and let's build a little log cabin.

Some of the how-to books on log cabins suggest starting with Lincoln Logs. If you are lucky, you can find them at yard sales and antiques shops. You can also make model logs out of small dry branches. Remember, everything is about patience.

Almost since the dawn of magazines there have been projects you can do at home. Today's supermarket newsstands brim with them. One of my favorites is the how-to article from *American Forestry* magazine of 1911:

How To Make Fir-Tree Furniture
K. WIREMAN

This amusing furniture is easy to make and will serve its purpose well during the holiday season. Here's what you need to make it: Ends of fir-tree branches, a paper of small fine pins, a sharp knife or razor blade, wire cutter, white shellac, and a small brush with which to apply it.

Gather ends of fir-tree branches five or six inches long, if possible. It is better to let them dry for a week or two, also. Take off all the needles, and if the branches become too dry soak them in water before starting to work.

For the ladder-back chair two strong sticks make the back. Decide on the height the seat is to be and put one stick across the two back sticks at this height and in the width you want for the chair. Push the pins through the upright and into the middle of the crosspiece. You will find it necessary to cut some of the pins short where two pins have to go in one crosspiece. When you do this, it is a good idea to make the holes first with a sharp pin, then substitute the cut pin. And where you can do so, cut the pin after it is through the upright, and then it is not so hard to push the blunt end through the soft pith of the crosspiece. It is easy if you put the head of the pin against the branch you are

The house under the holiday tree will be well-furnished with these fir-tree pieces. You can put them together in a jiffy!

working on and then press down the sticks upon it, as in this way the sticks will not be so apt to break and you can determine whether the pins are coming through in the right places. Only the heads of the pins show in the finished piece.

After arranging the two back pieces and the one crosspiece, fill in the back with four more crosspieces and one across the back legs. Next make front legs the proper height for the seat and join to back with two sticks in leg part, filling in the seat with crosspieces. Or you can make the seat before joining back and front together. The seat is the hardest to make, as it is necessary to have several pins along the side pieces, and it is for this reason that the wood should not be too dry. When finished, put chair on a level surface, straighten any crooked places, and shellac. Two coats may be necessary, as this makes the joints stay firm.

For the table and smaller chair, a piece of cardboard is used for the top and seat. Outline the edge with sticks for the table, leaving a small space at the corners to pin on legs. It is better to have the pins full length for the legs. Crosspieces around the bottom and uprights at each side make the table firm. Shellac the cardboard top with the sticks.

For the small chair it is not necessary to outline the edge of the seat. Make the upright crosspiece wider to the seat with gingham with a ruffle around the edge. This cover can be pinned or sewed on.

The bench has uprights like the chair, only farther apart, and the front legs are longer to give a place for arms. An upright is put in the middle back for firmness and the seat is made in two sections, joining the back and front. The decorative pieces are joined by pins at lower ends only. Put a temporary pin in the top of the lower one to hold them up and together, and let the upper ones fit under the crosspiece in back. Shellac all together. This will hold any part that does not bear strain. Remove the temporary pins after the shellac dries.

The lamp has three tips at the base for a stand and a paper shade held together by paste, the sticks being shellacked as in the other pieces.

And for those for whom all that making is just too much, this appeared a few issues later. It's about a man who found and collected alphabet letters grown on trees.

Alphabet Grown on Trees

H. E. ZIMMERMAN
from *American Forestry*, 1919

In the course of a number of years Mr. E. A. Miles, of Clifton Springs, New York, has collected one of the most unique alphabets in existence. In addition to the letters of the alphabet a complete set of numerals was also collected. The numerals and letters were all cut from trees, the numerals only having been found in the vicinity of Clifton Springs. There is but one root in the collection. In no instance have the letters or numerals been twisted into their present shape. They grew that way naturally. The letters are from the following places: A from Oshawa, Canada; B from Banff, Canada; C from near the summit of Mt. Tamalpais, California; D from Erie County, New York; E from Marilla, New York; F from Great Falls of the Potomac, near Washington, D. C.; G near Attica, New York; H near Clifton Springs, New York (this letter is the only one formed from a root); I from the grounds near the former home of William A. Wheeler, Malone, New York, former Vice-President of the United States; J from Grand Canyon of the Colorado, Arizona; K near Attica, New York; L from Lunday's Lane battlefield, Ontario, Canada; M near Attica, New York, while walking with his mother, a striking coincidence indeed, when it is remembered that the word "mother" begins with an "M"; N, which was the first one discovered, was found near Clifton Springs, New York; O and P were also found there; Q came from near the top of Mt. Lowe, California; R from near the Parliament buildings, Toronto, Canada; S near Clifton Springs, New York. On a visit to the tomb of Lincoln, Springfield, Illinois, Mr. Miles saw a gentleman trimming a tree near Lincoln's tomb. In one of the small branches cut away Mr. Miles saw a well-formed letter T. He got it for the mere asking. U is from Clifton Springs, New York; V is from Plains of Abraham, Quebec, Canada, where Wolf died; W near Attica, New York; X on Little Roundtop, Gettsburg, [sic] Pennsylvania; Y in the vicinity of Petersburg, Virginia, where the well-known tunnel was exploded in the Civil War, and Z near Attica, New York.

Formations from trees and shrubs growing on battlefields and places of historic interest in the United States and Canada, making a complete alphabet and numerals.

Are these articles better left in the bottom drawer of popular culture? No, they are important because they reflect a persisting need for the ephemeral: that which is not clearly in the service of the rational. There is a need for the other. It's part of the motion of life.

RUSTIC
REPLICAS

Here is some inspiration for making your own log cabin. George De Mille is the owner of Rustic Replicas in River Forest, Illinois, which designs and makes miniature log cabins, including do-it-yourself log-cabin kits. The kit contains 180 pieces, including cedar shingles, stones for the fireplace, plaster of paris for chinking, and detailed instructions. You can reach George at *cabinkit@aol.com* or check out his Web site at *www.rusticreplicas.com*.

LADDERS

Ladders are pure potential energy: they just stand there waiting for that moment when they feel the weight on the first rung, then the second, etc. Imagine being a ladder. It must be what a fireman feels like: a life of expectancy. A few ladders in the old books on cabins and pioneers are interesting variations on rustic or kiva ladders I have been used to building from saplings.

FURNITURE AND OTHER PROJECTS

Working with logs is cumbersome. Often they are heavy and clumsy and you need tools that are just outside the human scale. Oh, they say the pioneers just needed an axe, an adze, and an auger—and it is probably true. But the skills for using those tools easily are about as common as the words themselves.

When I have made log beds and lofts, I have usually worked with a local fence-post company that was set up with the size and power of tools beyond the set-up in my chair-making shop. I would draw up a careful set of plans and some drawings that indicated the diameter of the logs, the overall length, and the diameter and length of the tenons they would cut on the ends. I would also indicate where I wanted holes drilled. I would then go to the mill, where Bill and I selected and worked the few dozen pieces.

Here are a few of the projects that came out after sanding, assembly staining, sealing, and waxing. One of the first was an L-shaped loft for my children when we lived in New York City.

I made about a half-dozen of these, each quite customized to the room, windows, radiators, and temperaments of the children involved. The one below was particularly interesting because there was no ladder to get to the loft. The two brothers could climb the trees on the end and the little sister (whom I put in the loft for the picture) couldn't get up . . . yet! This became a jungle gym in the yard when the family moved out of their New York City apartment.

PHOTO COURTESY LYNNE REYNOLDS

Furniture is always a popular project. This scene of building camp furniture is from *Through the Wilds*, 1892.

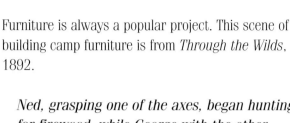

Ned, grasping one of the axes, began hunting for firewood, while George with the other felled some small forked maples. He cut four of these the proper length, and drove them into the ground two feet apart one way, and six feet the other. Then he cut two small sticks a couple of inches in diameter, two feet and six inches long, and placed them in the forks of the table-legs. After which he cut about ten small maples, there being plenty in the vicinity. The last he made a little over six feet long, flattening them on one side with the axe, and then laid them on the cross-pieces. A couple of alder withes, one bound around each end of the table, made the whole thing complete and ready for the dishes. The same arrangement along one side of the table, only lower, and with an extra pair of legs and cross-piece in the middle to resist the spring of the poles, finished the seat. "You would make a good wood butcher," said Ned, as he came up sweltering under a huge armful of wood. "I'll be hanged if you haven't dis-

played a good deal of ingenuity in the construction of that table and bench. Ever make one before?"

This sounds like an extravagant waste of wood on a very rickety set-up. It is presented to show that even in the good-old days bad ideas seemed to get around.

READING

**D**oing and making don't always mean constructing and working with tools in a workshop. The fundamental process is one of selection and arrangement. It is a dedication of time and interest. That can happen in many different ways and in many arenas of life.

Reading creates a shift in time (it slows down) and space—it takes the reader somewhere. First, take the pleasure of finding books somewhere, whether it be the library, the bookstore, or on-line. Once you find a book, spend your well-deserved time looking through them. Start at the back if you want, or just open a book and see where it takes you. It is great to spend an hour or two reading every day. You will find it a warm and comfortable pastime.

Two Great Reads from the *Log Cabin Living* Library

Shelters, Shacks, and Shanties, by D. C. Beard.
Meetings With Remarkable Trees, by Thomas Packenham.

DANCING: THE CABIN FEVER DANCE

H as the love of log cabins ever made you want to just get up and dance? Well, thanks to Brenda Jean Miller of Brookville, Pennsylvania, there is the Cabin Fever Dance.

DESCRIPTION: 2-Wall Line Dance
DIFFICULTY: Beginning
COUNT/STEPS: 40 Counts / 40 Steps
BPM: 153
TEACHING MUSIC: "I Love the Nightlife," Scooter Lee
DANCING MUSIC: "From Good to Bad to Worse to Gone"

1-8 LEFT WEAVE WITH HEEL GRINDS
1   Cross step RIGHT over Left
2   Step to the Left on LEFT, grinding Right heel and turning the toes to the right
3   Cross step RIGHT over Left
4   Step to the Left on LEFT, grinding Right heel and turning the toes to the right
5   Cross step RIGHT over Left
6   Step
7   Cross step RIGHT over Left
8   Step to the Left on LEFT, grinding Right heel and turning the toes to the right

9-16 STOMPS & HEEL CLICKS
1   Stomp slightly forward on RIGHT
2   Stomp LEFT next to Right
3   Click heels together
4   Click heels together
5   Stomp slightly forward on RIGHT
6   Stomp LEFT next to Right
7   Click heels together
8   Click heels together

17-24 VINE RIGHT WITH TOUCH, Hip Bumps
1   Step to the Right on RIGHT
2   Cross step LEFT behind Right
3   Step to the Right on RIGHT
4   Touch LEFT next to Right
5   Step to the Left on LEFT while bumping hips to the Left
6   Bump
7   Bump hips to the Right
8   Bump hips to the Right again

25-32 VINE LEFT WITH TOUCH, Hip Bumps
1   Step to the Left on LEFT
2   Cross step RIGHT behind Left
3   Step to the Left on LEFT
4   Touch RIGHT next to Left
5   Step to the Right on RIGHT while bumping hips to the Right
6   Bump hips to the Right again
7   Bump hips to the Left
8   Bump hips to the Left again

33-40   ROCK STEPS, STEP, 1/2 PIVOT LEFT, KICKS

1	Rock step forward on RIGHT
2	Rock back onto LEFT
3	Rock step back on RIGHT
4	Rock forward onto LEFT
5	Step forward on RIGHT
6	Pivot 1/2 turn to the Left
7	Kick RIGHT foot forward
8	Kick RIGHT foot forward

QUIL

THE
LOG CABIN
QUILT

The icon of the log cabin has long been popular among quilting circles across America. A log-cabin block is a classic quilting pattern based on rectangles added around a center square.

LEARNING
A SKILL

Knot tiers are people to envy. Not many people can tie a triple wello-haunch. It's never too late and it's always the right time to learn something new. This is not just for the skill you might learn but for the process that learning requires. Learning is a lifelong activity. We learn every day about something: traffic, sadness, new products, our health. This is involuntary learning. I recommend the simple pleasures of voluntary learning. Go right to the Boy Scout Handbook *or the* Girl Scout Handbook *and* pick a skill.

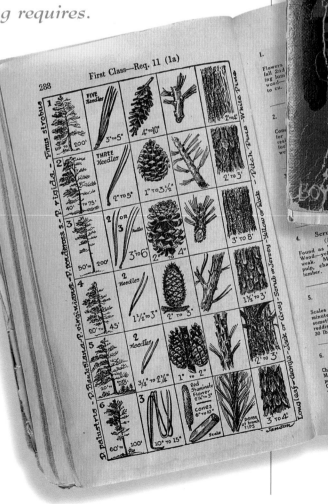

COLLECTING

 *athering objects around you is a time-honored way of spending time. In each object is the germ of another place or time. For the Log Cabin Living person, collections of postcards, old souvenirs, tools, or even old books on camping, nature, and trees can make life more vivid.*

Like a coral reef broken up by a wild storm, the log cabin survived in bits and pieces, as souvenirs, as miniatures, as furniture, and as yard accessories. Each part has the power to invoke the feeling of the whole. A good rustic chair or arbor can transport its user to another time.

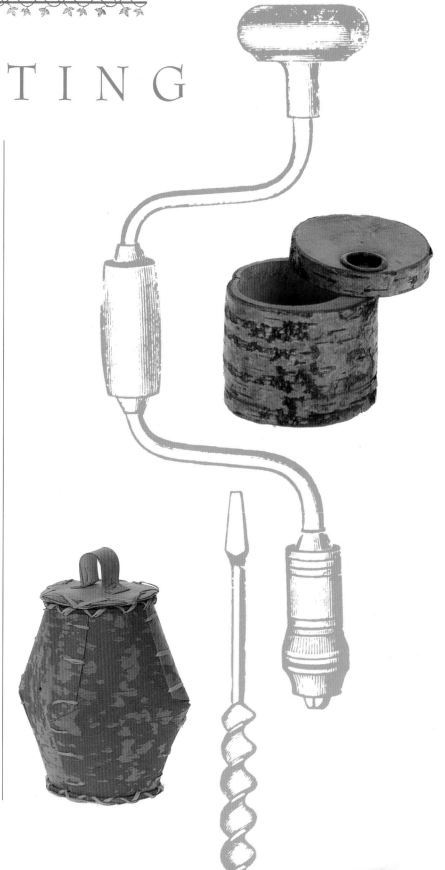

Log Cabin Collector
Wally Young

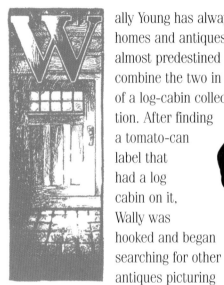

Wally Young has always loved log homes and antiques, so it was almost predestined that he would combine the two in the form of a log-cabin collection. After finding a tomato-can label that had a log cabin on it, Wally was hooked and began searching for other antiques picturing or shaped like log cabins. In four years, his collection has grown to over three hundred pieces. In addition to collecting, Wally and his wife, Susan, are Virginia dealers for Kuhns Bros. Log Homes, and they hope to display all of their pieces in their next log house. If you have a similar passion and would like to contact Wally, he can be reached at (540) 362-2789 or by e-mail at *loghomectr@aol.com*.

PHOTOS COURTESY KEVIN HURLEY

Souvenirs

 **T**he lingering power of the souvenir is hidden right in its name. From the French, it's "to remember" and from the earlier Latin "come back to mind."

❧ ❧ ❧

It's the same with log cabins. The product: the post-card, the balsam pillow, the striped camp blanket, the twig frame . . . that little antique chair, that birch-bark basket, that twig pen. They all do the same thing. They help move people from one place to another. Objects are our friends.

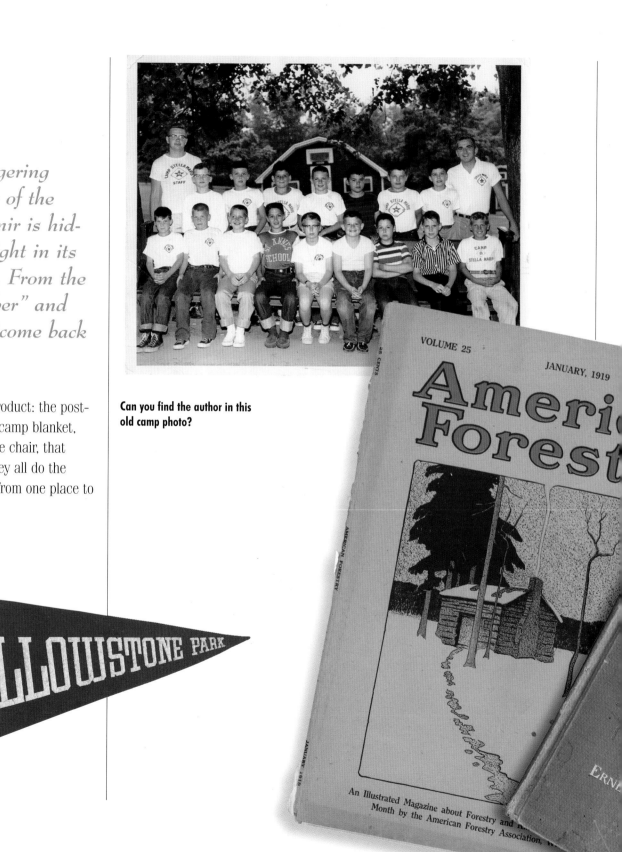

Can you find the author in this old camp photo?

VOLUME 25

JANUARY, 1919

America
Forest

An Illustrated Magazine about Forestry and
Month by the American Forestry Association.

YELLOWSTONE PARK

ERNE

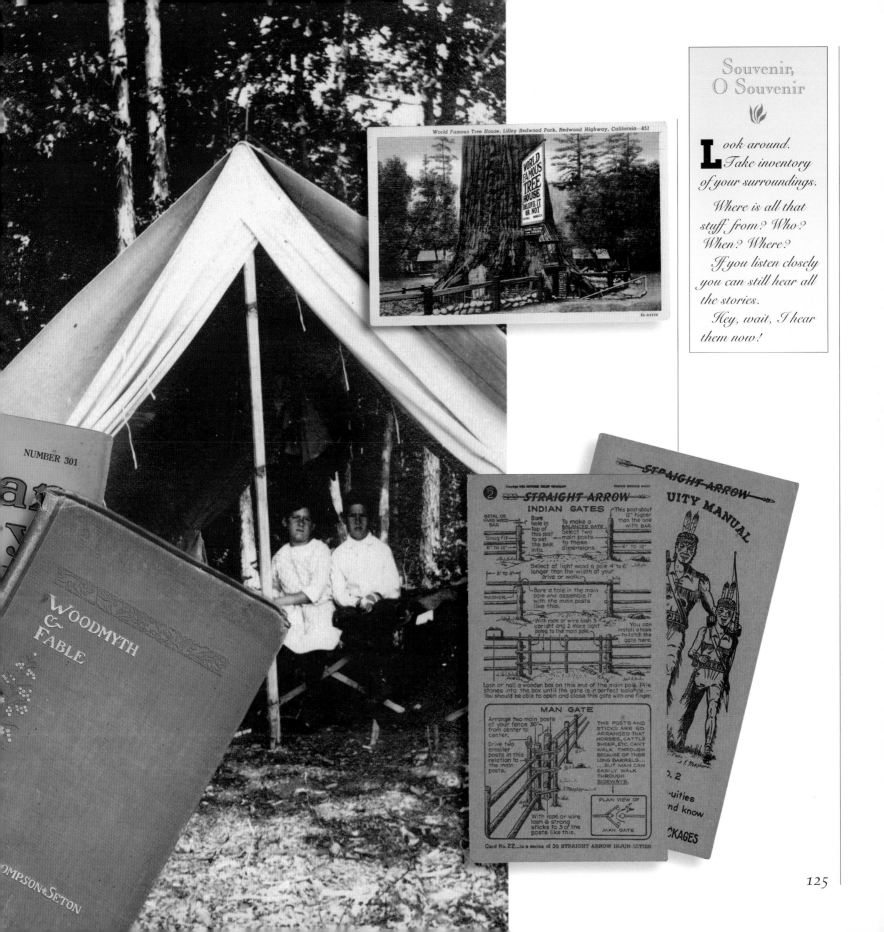

Souvenir,
O Souvenir

Look around. Take inventory of your surroundings.

Where is all that stuff from? Who? When? Where?

If you listen closely you can still hear all the stories.

Hey, wait, I hear them now!

World Famous Tree House, Lilley Redwood Park, Redwood Highway, California—851

NUMBER 301

WOODMYTH & FABLE

THOMPSON SETON

STRAIGHT ARROW
INDIAN GATES

MAN GATE

A Voice from the Web Offers This Little House Commentary

I was a child in the '70s and the books and life of Laura Ingalls Wilder were my whole world. The Little House on the Prairie *series was a staple, and in her first book,* Little House in the Big Woods, *the Ingalls family built their log cabin. There's an image in the first book, where Laura and her sister Mary are in the attic room playing. They sit and make believe amongst the pumpkins, veggies, and dried herbs. There is a feeling of bounty and it's all right there in their little home. At the same time the pumpkins are chairs to sit on to have tea.*

Even though the Ingalls lived in different kinds of dwellings throughout Laura's life, the log cabin for me was the most memorable. I associated log cabins with frontier life, coziness, family, simplicity, and grounding. There's something in my bones . . . something familiar and comforting about this structure. I think of fireplaces, windows with an orange glow, self-sufficiency, a pioneering spirit, and ancestry. As a child, this kind of life captured my imagination. I wore a prairie dress and bonnet, antique shoes, and carried my basket in hand. I hung out laundry to dry, played in a dilapidated barn, and fed our goats and chickens with an unparalleled enthusiasm. I enjoyed everything more in part because of these books. It was a huge part of my world. I wanted to be there. Even as an adult, I have found myself occasionally picking up one of those books, to be refreshed, to remember, to come home. The books remind me to be grateful, to take nothing for granted, and to enjoy everything: bare feet in the grass, an apple pie made with the last bits of sugar, the wind and sun, your favorite cup, and Pa's fiddle. As a child I aspired to be this, and the child grew to an adult. Some things have changed and others are lost, but it's good to remember. Sometimes I wish Laura had written more books about being an adult. It might be helpful at this time. I no longer wear a bonnet, but I know how to slow down sometimes, to be happy with just the moon and pine tree or a pizza made from scratch, and to keep the wheel turning. This is home to me.

EATING

*O*ne of the true joys of traveling is the never-ending search for food. Food is a barometer that indicates something about you and the people around you. It is interesting to use food as a guide to log cabins: old recipes, memories of camp food, and methods of cooking.

Methods

Baking in a Hole

Dig a hole in the ground about eighteen inches square and twelve inches deep. Place kindling in it and over the hole. Build a cob house by laying split wood sticks across, not touching each other, until you have a stack two feet high. Set fire to it and let it burn to coals. Cut up the meat, season it, and add a small piece of fat pork. Put it in a kettle, add water to cover, put on the lid, rake coals out of the hole, and put the kettle in. Shovel the coals around and over the kettle so it is covered with a few inches of earth. Let it sit overnight.

This is the way a traditional clambake is still prepared. True baked beans are also slow-cooked in an earthen bean pot (the forerunner of the Crock-Pot).

Cooking on a Stick

Although most of us think of marshmallows or shish kabab on the grill, there are several camp recipes that depend on meats and dough being skewered or wound around a stick. This is a way to be in touch with the entire cooking process. As an example, take a look at appalos in the old food glossary on page 130.

Foraging

Foraging has been a bit suspect since naturalist Euell Gibbons died of a heart attack on national television. There is something suspicious about being able to go right to Central Park and find edible plants. Many of us feel more comfortable paying money for every bit of food we get, knowing that it has been grown far away, treated with insecticides and preservatives, and shipped long distances at great cost. There are people who have returned to growing more of their own food or using local farmers' markets or asking the large food stores to buy from local farms. This is very much in the simple tradition of the log cabin. The system of agribusiness with super farms and complicated systems of handling and distributing was not available until this century.

No one today is suggesting a diet built around a few dominant foods, but there is a forager and cultivator tucked into all of us. Who among us hasn't had an herb garden? Even people who live on the sixteenth floor of a metropolitan apartment building have window boxes for herbs.

Cattail Salad

This salad was first made by Native Americans from the ivory-colored cattail shoots that came up in early spring. Pioneers copied and popularized this custom. Go to a swamp when the cattails are just beginning to send up new shoots. Cut off the shoots that are one to three inches long. Clean them so nothing but the solid ivory part remains. Cut the shoots into small pieces. Salt to taste.

Don't Try These at Home

Following are instructions from a few early-twentieth-century books for ways of cooking what used to be staples in the American diet.

Baking an Animal in Its Hide

If the animal is too large to bake whole, cut off what you want and sew it up in a piece of its hide. Line the hole with flat stones. Rake out coals and put meat in; cover with the green grass or leaves, coals and ashes, then build a fire on top. When done, remove the hide.

Baking in Clay

Dress the animal but leave the skin and hair or feathers on. If it is a large bird, cut off the head and feet and pinions, pull out the tail feathers, and cut off the tail (to get rid of oil sack). If you are cooking fish, do not scale. Stir clay in a pail of water until thick like porridge. Dip the bird in this, and repeat until it is a mass of clay. Lay this in the embers or ashes, being careful to dry the outside. Bake until the clay is almost burned to a brick. This mode of cooking should never be tried in regions where the clay is not real.

Rabbits and Squirrels

Rabbits and squirrels are pests to the farmer and, except in the spring of the year, are desirable food. The gray digger squirrel and the cottontail rabbit are abundant in many sections of the country. In utilizing such game for food, the camper not only adds variety to his diet in camp but performs a distinct service to the farmer.

1. Plain Fried Rabbit or Squirrel

Rabbits must be very tender for this purpose. Clean and cut into joints; soak for half an hour in salt and water (one tablespoon of salt to one quart of water), dip in flour, and fry in one-third cup of lard or substitute until brown.

2. Special Fried Rabbit or Squirrel

Here's another version of the recipe, reputed to be 200 years old (the recipe, not the rabbit), which includes nutmeg, cinnamon, and horseradish.

Cut up a jackrabbit or snowshoe rabbit into serving pieces and salt and pepper to taste. Melt a generous amount of butter in a large frying pan and brown all sides of the rabbit pieces well. Remove the rabbit meat from the pan and put into a baking pan with a cover. In the melted butter add one-half teaspoon of nutmeg, one-half teaspoon of cinnamon, and one or two teaspoons of powdered horseradish. Stir well and then pour on top of the rabbit pieces. Add one-half cup of water. Bake at 350 degrees for one hour. Take one tablespoon of flour and mix with three tablespoons of cold water until there are no lumps. Remove rabbit from pan and add flour mixture to remaining liquid in pan; stir well. Serve the rabbit with potatoes and gravy.

3. Stewed Rabbit

Clean, wash, cut into joints, and soak rabbit in salt and water (same proportion as fried). Put in kettle with cold water to cover, salt slightly, and stew until tender. Boiled onions (three medium-sized to one rabbit) may be added to this stew if desired.

You don't actually have to get into the kitchen to get the shift in perspective that unusual food can offer. Here's a short dictionary of food-related terms from the time of the pioneers, trappers, and mountain men. Let these words bathe you and carry you to a time and place when they were in common use.

Food Glossary

Appalos An early camp food made by skewering alternate pieces of lean meat and fat on a sharpened stick and roasting over a low fire. When it was possible to get them, pieces of potato or vegetable were mixed with the fat and the meat. This method of cooking was much used by many tribes of Indians as well as mountain men.

Boudins A buffalo gut containing chyme, cut into lengths about twenty-four inches long and roasted before a fire until crisp and sizzling.

Buffalo Cider The fluid found in the buffalo stomach used to quench thirst.

Dumpling Dust Flour. This term originated from the early practice of mixing dough by pouring water in a depression made in the flour while it was still in the sack, causing small puffs of dust. Both the term and practice are still used by North Woodsmen.

Dutch Oven A large kettle with three feet and a lid used for both cooking and baking.

Feast Cakes or Gordos Other terms for flapjacks, hotcakes, or pancakes.

Fizz-Pop A very early soda pop made by mixing a little vinegar and a spoon of sugar in a glass of fresh water. Just before drinking, mix in about a quarter of a spoon of soda. Also referred to as "shrub."

Galette A flour-water bread made into flat round cakes and fried in fat or baked before the open fire.

I Have a Grease Hunger An expression meaning "I am hungry for meat."

Grease and Beans A general expression meaning food.

Green Meat Meat that still had the animal heat in it.

Hump Ribs The small support ribs of the buffalo's hump.

Jerky Dried meat made by cutting meat into strips about 1 inch wide, 1/4 inch thick, and as long as possible. This was then sundried on racks often with a small hardwood fire under the meat to smoke it and to keep insects off it. In hot weather the meat would dry and be ready to use in three to four days.

To Larrupt To eat in a hasty and sloppy manner.

Larruping Good Anything that has an extra fine flavor.

Lumpy Dick An early pudding made by stirring dry flour into boiling milk until thick, then serving with sweet milk and molasses or sugar.

FROM THE AMERICAN MOUNTAIN MEN

In Linda Runyon's years in the woods as a home-steader in the Adirondacks, she learned a lot about natural edibles:

As I began to learn more about winter, I decided to can my wild foods during the summer for use later in the year. We had a seven-and-a-half-foot insulated refrigerator pit where they would keep well. I trusted my judgment on this, for I had canned many times in my "city life." So after a long canning season I had 420 jars of campfire-canned foods in my storehouse.

Winter came, and we were thrilled to eat our canned foods—cattails, milkweed, lamb's quarters, blueberries, and strawberries. Everything was delicious. Then, three weeks of twenty- to forty-below temperatures began. A blizzard snowed us in, but I knew we had plenty of food. The winds howled, the snow swirled, and when morning came, the refrigerator pit had to be dug out. When the roof was uncovered, I opened the pit and climbed down the ladder with my lantern in hand. My eyes blinked in disbelief. It seemed as if every one of the jars had exploded. I was in a complete panic. I grabbed the snow shovel and began to scoop the jars off the shelves to find ones that had just begun to freeze. Alas, there were but a few jars with small cracks or pushed-up lids.

Reconstituted dried leaves and vegetables and flour became our immediate food sources. We even ground bark into flour or brewed it for teas. Somehow we survived. I look back now and say that it was this experience that led me to write my book. (See page 96.)

VACATIONING

In addition to some of the great camps already listed, vacationing at many places across the country can put you in the Log Cabin Living *frame of mind. Here are three such places in the West.*

The Out'n'About Treehouse Institute & Treesort

300 Page Creek Road
Cave Junction, Oregon 97523
(800) 200-5484
www.treehouses.com

There are many adventurous vacation sites in southern Oregon, but only one where you can truly go out on a limb.

Out'n'About Treesort has gone a long way—all the way up into the branches of an oak grove among the Siskiyou Mountains—to provide a unique opportunity for visitors to get back to their rustic roots.

To stay at the resort, you have to become a Tree Musketeer and vow to protect the trees and the tree-houses, becoming a friend of the trees. Proprietor Michael Garnier administers the vow and says, "Any friend of the trees and treehouses is a friend of mine, and therefore welcome to stay overnight."

Fashioned primarily of Douglas fir poles and rough-cut beams, the treehouses feature single-wall construction, in keeping with the "we're all kids here" theme.

UNDERCUT OF A 12 FT. WASHINGTON DOUGLAS FIR TREE. 12 FT. 600 - SORRENSON PHOTO PUB BY ELLIS

The resort offers a Treeroom Schoolhouse Suite (complete with a queen bed, loft, kitchenette, and a full bath), the Swiss Family Complex (connected by a swinging bridge), the Peacock Perch (their tallest treehouse), a Cavaltree Fort, a Treepee, and a two-story luxury cabin.

While staying at the Treesort, guests can attend the Treehouse Institute, which offers instruction in the basic engineering, design, and construction methods for building treehouses, as well as other classes involving crafts (mask making, pottery, whittling, etc.), the performing arts (acting, costuming, etc.), physical education (tree climbing, kayaking, swimming, etc.), equestrianism, and home economics (gardening, chicken feeding, egg collecting, etc.).

More information, including great pictures of the treehouses, can be found on their Web site.

PHOTOS COURTESY THE OUT 'N' ABOUT
TREEHOUSE INSTITUTE AND TREESORT

The Lodge at Skylonda

16350 Skyline Boulevard
Woodside, California 94062
(800) 851-2222

Named for the nineteenth-century logging mill that once occupied the site, The Lodge at Skylonda is the only resort if its kind. It is nestled in northern California's majestic redwood forest and was created to give guests a respite from the complexities of daily living.

The retreat is a three-story log-and-stone structure that is designed to be a rejuvenating experience for the mind, body, and spirit. It offers sixteen guest rooms featuring custom-made beds and other amenities.

Highlights include hiking trails through the redwoods and a full-service spa.

Post Ranch Inn

Highway One
Post Office Box 219
Big Sur, California
93920
(800) 527-2200

In keeping with the strong historical connection to the region, the Post Ranch Inn's theme is local tradition and culture.

Designed by architect G. K. Muennig with the preservation of the local surroundings uppermost in mind, the inn greets guests with rustic elegance and a sense of intimacy. It is comprised of two lodges and thirty custom guest units featuring four distinct styles, including seven treehouse units. All the units feature spectacular shoreline and mountain views.

Part Four

LIVING LOGSTYLE TODAY

he range of log residence work today is dizzying, from modest cabins to immodest mansions, retirement homes, vacation homes, starter homes, and trophy homes. About two billion dollars a year are spent on building log homes. Some are handcrafted, others are precut, and still others are salvaged and restored.

Salvaged, Relocated, and Restored

Some of the more unusual log homes, and by no means the least expensive, are those that have been retrieved or salvaged from one place and repaired and reerected another place. There are a dozen small companies that specialize in this kind of work. An example of this is a cabin that was called the Poor House on a remote piece of land in rural Kentucky. It had been built in the 1850s and lived in until the 1970s. Timber and Stone of Fredericksburg, Texas, purchased it and moved it to Houston, where it became the centerpiece of a 2,000-square-foot rock-and-log complex.

PHOTOS COURTESY TIMBER AND STONE

The new complex after Timber and Stone's renovation.

The Poor House
before relocation.

Similarly, in Wyoming Kim Rathmann and her husband started with a few small cabins, then restored and expanded over a six-year period:

We have spent the last six years refurbishing a one-hundred-year-old cabin in Jackson Hole, Wyoming. We took the original structure of about 1,400 square feet, which was an original homesteader cabin that had been combined with an old log chapel, and turned it into a 3,600-square-foot home. The cabin is located in Grand Teton National Park. We did everything by hand and spent many hours loving, hating, laughing, and crying through the project. When we first began construction, we hired an architect to prepare drawings and obtain building permits. However, as the project got under way, we quickly realized that what was on paper had no basis in the reality of day-to-day operation. So, we threw out the drawings and I designed the structure as we went.

PHOTOS COURTESY KIM RATHMANN

In addition to people restoring existing cabins, there are those who are building the future by reclaiming the past. Ed Knapp, of Vintage Beams in Sylva, North Carolina, is committed to preserving the historic charm of the past and the natural forest resources of the future by reclaiming antique timbers for use in building today. Their timbers originate from logs cut from old-growth forests over 100 years ago and have been reclaimed from all over the United States and, most recently, China and Mexico. He can be contacted at (704) 586-0755, P.O. Box 548, Sylva, North Carolina 28779.

PHOTOS COURTESY VINTAGE BEAMS

Contemporary Examples

In these homes, there is an architectural and textural reference point to help direct the new shape of the structure. But in another vein of contemporary log homes, the owner and the architect have the chance to create those reference points. Most contemporary architects have created log residences in their career. And a few, like David Sellers of Vermont, have specialized in it.

Designed by Sellers, the Smith Lodge in Vermont is the fifth and most evolved in a series of structures crafted from local and native materials. These materials were shaped by natural forces over time and expressed as the fabric of space definition and structure. Here, massive sugar maples cut from the site were gently laid down with a crane and relocated in the house as vertical structure with the bark— selected branches, bugs, and all. This all aligns with

David's philosophy of replacing what he sees as the carelessness and cheapness of America's current construction with long-term vitality, uniqueness, regional identity, and feisty creativity. Sellers is currently designing the Gesundheit Institute, Patch Adams' innovative humorous hospital (West Virginia), a dormitory for the Putney School (Vermont), a family ski lodge (Vermont), and a Museum of Industrial History (Middlebury, Vermont).

Another example of a contemporary great camp is the Big Cedar Lodge resort owned by Bass Pro Shops.

PHOTO BY JARED POLESKY,
COURTESY SELLERS & CO.

142

Big Cedar Lodge.

Handcrafted

Yet a third form of the contemporary log home is the handcrafted home. Here, the very skilled log builder often works directly with the client. The final structure is often built at the handcrafter's shop and then disassembled and reassembled on the client's site. Beaver Creek Log Homes in Oneida, New York, is a great example.

PHOTOS COURTESY BEAVER CREEK LOG HOMES

FURNITURE

I have been making rustic furniture every day for the last twenty years. For a while it seemed that I was a furniture maker. In a way, that was so, but, more importantly, I see now that I was working rustic.

Rustic is work in the twilight . . . that light between day and night, between worlds. The world looks different in twilight, and the same is true with rustic. It is more an attitude toward making than a set body of designs and techniques.

The following examples are about people who have been lured into the twilight and have found pleasure and fulfillment in a very ancient activity . . . making something special out of something ordinary. This is magic realism, revealing of the sacred in the mundane. Here are objects—chairs, benches, and utensils—made from wood hardly useful as kindling. With attention, time, and skill, craftspeople have breathed a kind of magic into this useless wood.

There is an enduring lure in the nature of rustic. Like the trees in the woods, it beckons and welcomes. The makers here are adventurers and wanderers, exploring the erratic nature of trees and their homegrown sense of beauty.

FOREST LOVESEAT BY LIZ HUNT (614) 459-1551

RUSTIC CABINET BY TOM PHILLIPS (518) 359-9648

JAKE LEMON FURNITURE (208) 788-3004

149

RUSTIC TABLE AND DETAIL ON FACING PAGE BY PAUL GALANTE

ROBERT DOYLE

153

BIRCH CORNER CABINET.
BARRY GREGSON (518) 532-9384

No. 178 **Desk**
        Top 27 x 50 inches   **Price $75.00**
No. 192 **Table**
        Oak top 28 x 48 inches. Finished Golden Oak   **Price $35.00**
No. 205 **Muffin Stand**
        Height 38 inches   **Price $ 7.00**

No. 230 **Magazine Rack Price $12.00**
        Height 35 inches, width 26 inches
No. 245 **Paper Basket   Price $ 4.00**
        Size 12 x 12 inches, height 13 inches
No. 350 **Canes, per dozen Price $ 8.00**
No. 352 **Cane Stand   Price $ 3.50**
        Height 31 inches

RESOURCES

So many of us are used to bibliographies, supply lists, tool lists, workshop lists, and so forth, that resources seem to be very matter-of-fact. Actually they are not. Resources, far from being a monument to thoroughness or scholarship, can, in some hands, be a vehicle to places known, unknown, and pleasantly unexpected. This happened a lot during the research for this book. The greatest pleasure in this process was getting lost. It happened in books, on the internet, and in conversations. I hope you enjoy the same pleasures.

Books for Getting into the Log Cabin Experience

Finding many of these books is a project unto itself. Many are out of print and can be found in the camping, nature, or architecture section of used bookstores.

Studying Historical Sources

Gilborn, Craig. *Adirondack Furniture and the Rustic Tradition*. New York: Harry Abrams, 1987.

This is an essential book to help understand the major historical references for today's rustic furniture revival. Gilborn is a thorough and careful researcher.

Jordan, Terry G., and Matti Kaups. *The American Backwoods Frontier: An Ethnic and Ecological Interpretation*. Baltimore: Johns Hopkins Press, 1989.

This is the definitive book on the history and movement of the pioneers across the country. It is a semi-academic piece of work spending too much time and evidence refuting earlier theories. It is best and inspiring when it pioneers its own territory. Jordan has been visiting and photographing log cabins for thirty years and writes with a pleasant air of authority. He has written the two books that follow, and they are more specialized and may be of interest to people in the West and in Texas.

———. *The Mountain West: Interpreting the Folk Landscape.* Baltimore: Johns Hopkins University Press, 1997.

Jordan and others make the case that there is really not just one Old West, there are "multiple Wests," each cluster defined by differing forms of persisting ethnicity and the slightly dueling forces of the need for continuity of cultural forms and the need to adapt and innovate with them in specific circumstances. The collection of pictures Jordan has taken and collected are an extra bonus to his scholarship.

———. *Texas Log Buildings: A Folk Architecture*. Austin: University of Texas Press, 1978.

Jordan thoroughly documents and discusses the various forms of log structures and outbuildings in his home state of Texas. As in his other books, the photographs, references, and bibliography are excellent and provocative for more research.

Kaiser, Harvey. *Great Camps of the Adirondacks*. Boston: Godine, 1982. This is the definitive book on the great-camp era. Kaiser worked years on its preparation.

Weslager, C. A. *The Log Cabin in America—from Pioneer Days to the Present*. New Brunswick, New Jersey: Rutgers University Press, 1969.

This is a fundamental text on the subject. Weslager's devotion to the subject is evident on every page.

Deepening Your Appreciation of Trees, Nature, and Wilderness

Packenham, Thomas. *Meetings with Remarkable Trees*. New York: Random House, 1996.

A big picture book of affection and magic that gathers sixty specimen trees not by "families" but by the way they seem to move the human spirit.

Altman, Nathaniel. *Sacred Trees*. San Francisco: Sierra Club, 1994.

This is a nice, steady, wide-ranging book on the beliefs about trees throughout contemporary and historical primitive cultures. It's a very good reference but not terribly passionate.

Harrison, Robert Pogue. *Forests: The Shadow of Civilization*. Chicago: University of Chicago Press, 1992.

A dense but rich and intellectual exploration of the darker side of forests.

Nash, Roderick. *Wilderness and the American Experience*. Revised. New Haven, Connecticut: Yale Press, 1973.

An essential text to understanding the thinking and changes in thinking that contributed to the current configuration of public lands, parks, and the various environmental laws. Wilderness went from being the terrifying abode of the unknown to the place man sought for spiritual renewal. These changes had profound social and political manifestations. Nash develops all this quite fully.

Perlman, Michael. *The Power of Trees: The Reforesting of the Soul*. Woodstock, Connecticut: Spring Publications, 1994.

This is a pioneering book into the psychology of trees and being with trees. It has certain organizational challenges but is a rich source of information and ways of thinking.

Better Understanding the American Experience

Bettmann, Otto. *The Good Old Days—They Were Terrible*. New York: Random House, 1974.

Boorstin, Daniel. *The Exploring Spirit: America and the World Then and Now*. New York: Random House, 1976.

A brief chatty essay Boorstin prepared for the BBC where he elaborates on the ideas of verges and distinguishes the explorer from the discoverer.

———. *The Americans: The Democratic Experience*. New York: Random House, 1973. The last part of Boorstin's excellent survey of American history.

Kouwenhoven, John A. *The Beer Can by the Highway: Essays on What's American about America*. Baltimore: Johns Hopkins, 1988.

His last essay, which gives the book its title, is appropriate to pioneers and the frontier.

Orvell, Miles. *The Real Thing: Imitation and Authenticity in American Culture, 1880–1940*. Chapel Hill, North Carolina: University of North Carolina Press, 1995.

Shi, David E. *In Search of the Simple Life*. Salt Lake City: Gibbs Smith, Publisher, 1986. A good solid reader of excerpted primary materials of the way leaders and thinkers have wrestled with the fundamental American experience of consumption.

Getting Ideas about Log Style

Boyer, Marie-Frances. *Cabin Fever: Sheds and Shelters, Huts and Hideaways*. New York: Thames and Hudson, 1993.

Carley, Rachel. *Cabin Fever: Rustic Style Comes Home*. New York: Simon & Schuster, 1998.

Flood, Elizabeth Clair. *Rocky Mountain Home: Spirited Western Hideaways*. Salt Lake City: Gibbs Smith, Publisher, 1996.

O'Leary, Ann. *Adirondack Style*. New York: Random House, 1998.

Thiede, Arthur, and Cindy Teipner Thiede. *Hands-On Log Homes*. Salt Lake City: Gibbs Smith, Publisher, 1998.

A book filled with log homes that reflect the personalities and lifestyles of their owners. The Thiedes have become the documentarians of contemporary log-home living. They have done two earlier books listed below that feed the growing appetite for pictures and information.

———. *The Log Home Book: Design, Past and Present*. Salt Lake City: Gibbs Smith, Publisher, 1993.

———. *American Log Homes*. Salt Lake City: Gibbs Smith, Publisher, 1986.

Charming Books with Beautiful Illustrations

Bruyere, Christian, and Robert Inwood. *In Harmony with Nature: Creative Country Construction*. New York: Drake, 1975.

This is from the hippie-to-the-woods era and is well written with period drawings that look like they could have been done by a young and straight R. Cobb. There are several details in the drawings and writing that make the book almost classically antiquarian. I particularly like the bottle-masonry project and have plans to use all those blue ginseng tea bottles I have been saving.

Sloane, Eric. *Diary of an Early American Boy*. New York: Ballantine Books, 1965.

An illustrated and reconstructed life story from a true diary of a young boy in 1805.

———. *A Museum of Early American Tools*. New York: Ballantine, 1964.

A good introduction to the tools and ways of thinking about tools in pre-industrial America. There is also a museum of his work, the Sloane-Stanley Museum in Kent, Connecticut, that is well worth the visit. It is open mid-May through October. (860) 566-3005.

Building Log Cabins and Getting Back to Nature

Aldrich, Chilson D. *The Real Log Cabin*. New York: Macmillan, 1928.

A book by an architect who has devoted himself exclusively to designing and building log cabins. The introduction is charming and encouraging. Basically, he says carpe diem. Dream of your log cabin, then build it. I like chapter sixteen on log-cabin furniture. Chilson brings an educated eye and a sense of design to the cabin and offers several levels of appropriate carpentry from "haywire and gunnysack to modest cabinetry." This book has been reprinted.

Bealer, Alex W., and John O. Ellis. *The Log Cabin: Homes of the North American Wilderness*. Barre, Massachusetts: Barre Publishing, 1978.

A good clear introduction to the history and styles and tools of log cabins. This was written mostly as a historical survey with a very slight chapter on the revival.

Cheley, Frank H., and Philip D. Fagans, eds. *The Camper's Guide*. New York: Blue Ribbon Books, 1939.

This is a good collection of woodcraft information based on scouting but suitable for regular campers. I like the very thorough section on camp cookery.

Clemson, Donovan. *Living with Logs*. Saanichton, British Columbia: Hancock House Publishers, 1974.

Ninety-four pages of moody travelogue that includes black-and-white photographs of log buildings and rail fences in British Columbia. A very charming and personal book.

Hunt, W. Ben. *Rustic Construction*. Milwaukee: Bruce Publishing, 1939.

Ben Hunt is one of those legendary outdoorsmen. He was a Roy Rogers–Gene Autry kind of guy. He was an artist and teacher who knew how to pass on his enthusiasm for woodcraft in both his words and drawings. This book was reprinted by Macmillan in 1974 along with the one below.

———. *How to Build and Furnish a Log Cabin*. New York: Macmillan, 1974.

I also have a few copies of his *The Complete How-to Book of Indiancraft,* which has a collection of projects in which Dr. Freud might be interested.

Leitch, William C. *Hand-Hewn.* San Francisco: Chronicle Books, 1976.

A very inviting mix of technique, terms, and inspiration. Leitch credits Rutstrum's work and sees himself in the same lineage, though more contemporary.

Meinecke, Conrad E. *Cabin Craft and Outdoor Living*. Buffalo, New York: Foster and Stewart, 1947.

This seems to be a sequel to his earlier book *Your Camp in the Woods* (1945), republished by Bonanza Books in 1979. Meinecke is half-preacher, half-

nasty scoutmaster urging us to the woods for health and self-repair. He gets misty-eyed over his childhood acquaintance, Necktie Jim the good Indian, and rails against the softness of America. This is part of the John Wayne log-cabin literature where the last of the real men yell at the rest of us. This is pleasantly eccentric and there's one racy drawing of a lady taking a shower in the woods. The story of Necktie Jim is a great piece of gooey nostalgia. In both his books there are very interesting drawings of suggested furniture, which are interesting because they are country rustic based on the way trees grow and use very simple tools.

Nearing, Helen and Scott. *Living the Good Life: How to Live Sanely and Simply in a Troubled World*. New York: Schocken Books, 1970.

Popular Science Monthly editorial staff. *How To Build Cabins, Lodges, and Bungalows*. New York: Popular Science, 1934, 1946.

This is a great introduction to the technical aspects of log-cabin building with attention to commercial as well as residential uses. This is not at all old style. They use the most up-to-date materials and techniques and talk about precut log cabins and log siding. There is even a section about the log cabin in the city. This book has worn very well in fifty years. The drawings are still very clear and helpful.

Rutstrum, Calvin. *The*

Wilderness Cabin. New York: Macmillan, 1961.

A solid, short, no-nonsense book by a true contemporary woodsman. It is important because it reflects ways of thinking and building that span the mid-twentieth century.

Seton, Ernest Thompson. *Woodmyth and Fable*. New York: The Century Co., 1903.

Seton compiled the text and made very fetching illustrations for this 181-page book. It reads like an American *Grimm Brothers' Fairy Tales*, and the stories take a bit of time to unravel. The drawings are in several different styles and the whole book makes for a dreamlike experience. Its purpose is not quite clear, but it seems to touch the reader.

———. *The Book of Woodcraft*. Garden City, New York: Doubleday Page & Co., 1912.

This is another handbook of woodland ways based on friendly Indian lore. It includes bird, tree, and mushroom identification and a very well-developed section on camp games and stories. I find these interesting because we don't do such things any more as they take so much real time!

Making Furniture from Trees

Alexander, John. *How to Build a Chair from a Tree*. Newtown, Connecticut: Taunton Press, 1981.

Brown, John. *Welsh Stick Chairs*. Fresno, California: Linden Publishing, 1996.

Langsner, Drew. *Green Woodworking*. Asheville, North Carolina: Lark, 1995.

Mack, Daniel. *Making Rustic Furniture*. Asheville, North Carolina: Sterling/Lark, 1992.

———. *The Rustic Furniture Companion*. Asheville, North Carolina: Sterling/Lark, 1996.

———. *Simple Rustic Furniture*. Asheville, North Carolina: Lark, 1999.

Vintage and Reprint Books

Beard, Daniel Carter. *American Boys Handbook*. Jaffrey, New Hampshire: Godine, 1983.

———. *Shelters, Shacks, and Shanties*. New York: Scribner's, 1914.

Camp Buildings and Scout Shelters. BSA Service Library No. 3341, 1929.

Hasluck, Paul N. *Rustic Carpentry*. New York: Funk and Wagnalls, 1901.

Linoff, Victor, ed. *Rustic Hickory Furniture Company Porch, Lawn, and Cottage Furniture*. New York: Dover Publications, 1991.

Old Hickory Porch and Garden Furniture Catalog, 1901.

Wicks, William S. *Log Cabins and Cottages: How to Build and Furnish Them*. New York: Forest and Stream, 1920.

Related Books

Alexander, Christopher, et al. *Pattern Language: Towns, Buildings, Construction.* New York: Oxford Books, 1977.

A very important exploration of why some buildings "feel" right.

Bachelard, Gaston. *Poetics of Space.* Boston: Beacon Press, 1994.

————. *Psychoanalysis of Fire.* Boston: Beacon Press, 1965.

Drinkard, G. Lawson. *Hiding in a Fort: Backyard Retreats for Kids.* Salt Lake City: Gibbs Smith, Publisher, 1999.

Hyde, Lewis. *The Trickster Makes the World.* New York: Farrar, Strauss, Giroux, 1998.

Langdon, Philip. *American Houses.* New York: Stewart, Tabori, Chang, 1987.

Lawlor, Anthony. *The Temple in the House, Finding the Sacred in Everyday Architecture.* New York: Tarchner, 1994.

Marcus, Clare Cooper. *Home as Mirror of Self: Exploring the Deeper Meaning of Home.* Berkeley, California: Conari Press, 1997.

Miller, Perry. *Errand into the Wilderness.* Boston: Harvard University Press, 1956.

Monroe, Jean. *First Houses: Native American Homes and Sacred Structures.* Boston: Houghton Mifflin, 1993.

Rykwert, Joseph. *Adam's House in Paradise.* New York: The Museum of Modern Art, 1972.

Walker, Lester. *Housebuilding for Children.* Woodstock, New York: Overlook Press, 1977.

Other Resources

Besides books, there are several other ways to get more about the log-cabin experience. The Internet is a bottomless, ever-changing source of information. As good surfers know, the links at one site will probably take you on a journey to several unexpected places.

A key log-home Internet site is http://www.woodworking.com/loghomes/

They have a Q&A forum that is very informative, as well as listings of makers and schools.

Schools/Workshops

Here are the addresses of a few of the schools around North America and a few other places where log-interested people can get their hands on some wood in the good company of like-minded people.

Robert W. Chambers
N8203 1130th Street
River Falls, Wisconsin 54022
715-425-1739
715-425-1746 fax
E-mail: robert@logbuilding.org

The Pat Wolfe Log Building School
RR#3
Ashton, Ontario, Canada
K0A 1B0
613-253-0631
613-253-2604 fax
Web site:
http://www.igs.net/~pwolfe/

Log House Builders Association of North America
Skip Ellsworth
22203 State Route 203
Monroe, Washington 98272
Web site: http://www.premier1.net/~loghouse/

Heartwood School
Johnson Hill Road
Washington, Massachusetts 01223
413-623-6677
413-623-0277 fax
Web site: http://www.heartwoodschool.com/

Country Workshops
90 Mill Creek Road
Marshall, North Carolina 28753
704-656-2280
E-mail: langsner@countryworkshops.org

Daniel Mack Rustic Furnishings Workshops
14 Welling Avenue
Warwick, New York 10990
914-986-7293
E-mail: rustic@warwick.net
Web site: http://www.danielmack.com

Tools

The Electronic Neanderthal is the major Internet site: http://www.cs.cmu.edu/~alf/en/

Early American Industries Association
P.O. Box 143
Delmar, New York 12054
518-439-1066 fax
Web site: http://ourworld.compuserve.com/homepages/Old_tools/about.htm

Lee Valley Tools has a very good collection of hand and power tools for the rustic and log builder:
Lee Valley Tools Ltd.
12 East River Street
P.O. Box 1780
Ogdensburg, New York 13669-6780
Web site: http://www.leevalley.com/

Museums and Lodges

For the *Log Cabin Living* traveler, there are museums and resorts all over the country. Here are just a few:

Adirondack Museum
P.O. Box 99
Blue Mountain Lake, New York 12812
518-353-7311
Web site: http://www.adkmuseum.org/

Buffalo Bill Museum
720 Sheridan Avenue
Cody, Wyoming 82414
307-587-4771

Henry Ford Museum
20900 Oakwood Boulevard
Dearborn, Michigan 48121
313-271-1620

Shelburne Museum
P.O. Box 10, Route 7
Shelburne, Vermont 05482
802-985-3344

Western Heritage Center
2822 Montana Avenue
Billings, Montana 59101
406-256-6809